A History of the Jewish People

Volume I

This classic work explores the seminal early periods of Jewish history. The destruction of Jerusalem in 586 B.C. by the army of Nebuchadrezzar marks a radical turning point in the life of the people of Jehovah, for then the history of the Hebrew state and monarchy ends, and Jewish history as the record, not of a nation but of the scattered, oppressed remnants of the Jewish people, begins. Until comparatively recently, the four centuries which followed the destruction of Jerusalem have been regarded as the least important of those which constitute the background of the Bible. Modern critical study, however, has revealed their supreme importance. To the student of the Old Testament they are of the deepest interest, for they witnessed for the first time the popular acceptance of the principles enunciated by the pre-exilic prophets, and the remarkable expansion and application of the ceremonial law. It is now generally accepted that more than half of the literature of the Old Testament comes from this period. Among the subjects dealt with in this volume are the dispersion of the Jews; the Jewish exiles in Babylon; the literary activity of the exiles; the revival of the Jewish community in Palestine; the building of the temple, the institution of the priestly law; Jewish life in Egypt and Palestine; the conquests of Alexander and different currents of Jewish thought, ending with the re-dedication of the temple, the reunion of the Jewish people, and a foretaste of national independence.

A History of the Jewish People

Volume I

From the Babylon, Persian, and Greek Periods

Charles Foster Kent

Taylor & Francis Group
LONDON AND NEW YORK

First published in 2005 by
Kegan Paul International

This edition first published in 2011 by
Routledge
2 Park Square, Milton Park, Abingdon, Oxfordshire OX14 4RN

Simultaneously published in the USA and Canada
by Routledge
711 Third Avenue, New York, NY 10017

First issued in paperback 2016

Routledge is an imprint of the Taylor & Francis Group, an informa business

© Kegan Paul, 2006

All rights reserved. No part of this book may be reprinted or reproduced or utilised in any form or by any electronic, mechanical, or other means, now known or hereafter invented, including photocopying and recording, or in any information storage or retrieval system, without permission in writing from the publishers.

British Library Cataloguing in Publication Data
A catalogue record for this book is available from the British Library

ISBN 13: 978-1-138-97618-4 (pbk)
ISBN 13: 978-0-7103-1094-1 (hbk)

Publisher's Note
The publisher has gone to great lengths to ensure the quality of this reprint but points out that some imperfections in the original copies may be apparent. The publisher has made every effort to contact original copyright holders and would welcome correspondence from those they have been unable to trace.

PREFACE

THE division of the Hebrew kingdom at the death of Solomon turned the courses of Hebrew life and thought into such entirely new channels that that which precedes and that which follows this eventful act constitute, in a sense, two independent historical units. Both, however, are parts of an organic whole, and therefore our knowledge of one remains incomplete without a familiarity with the other. Recognizing that many threads were necessarily left loose, and that many conclusions, especially in the analysis of the historical sources, were stated without complete proof, it was with great hesitation that the first volume was submitted to the public. Its aims, however, have been so generously appreciated by all classes of Bible students that it is with keen pleasure that I now endeavor to redeem the implied promise, and gather up these loose threads by presenting the subsequent development of the history, since this itself constitutes the most satisfactory and final proof of the conclusions previously offered. Thus, for example, in the full light of the reformation of Josiah, the peculiar ideas of the Deuteronomic editor of Judges and Samuel are clearly intelligible, and the inconsistencies in these books, which at first seem so glaring, disappear in the true perspective of history. During the prophetic period also the great religious truths, heretofore found only in germ, unfold, making this, of all Semitic antiquity, the era unquestionably the richest in its intellectual and spiritual development.

While the determination to limit the present volume to the length prescribed by the wants of the busy reader has been persistently adhered to, the aim has been so to introduce him to the character, work, and essential teachings of each of the prophets that he may find in their recorded words that reality and meaning which are impossible without a clear understanding of their historical background.

A detailed critical analysis of the different prophetical books, which are the main historical sources for the various periods, has not been attempted, since the sections whose date and authorship are in question fortunately do not contain data of sufficient importance to modify materially our conception of the history; and therefore such a treatment would be aside from the purpose of the present work, which deals primarily with the life of the Hebrew people in its political, social, and religious aspects rather than with their literary products.

The course of the development of Hebrew history was determined so largely by the influence of the two great world-powers, Assyria and Babylonia, that they suggest the most practical division into periods. Before the advent of Assyria the histories of the two Hebrew kingdoms ran closely parallel and therefore they have been considered together. Subsequently they

PREFACE

were separated so widely that they have been treated independently. References to sections, preceded by the Roman numeral I., refer to the first volume of this history, which treats of the period included between the settlement in Canaan and the division of the kingdom.

Trusting that this work will prove to many only a starting-point for a more detailed study of the variety of interesting problems which arise in connection with each chapter, I have given in the Appendix a full list of references to the leading authorities. The bibliography therein contained also suggests the previous writers to whom I am indebted.

In the same connection I take pleasure in acknowledging a more personal indebtedness to Professor Frank K. Sanders, Ph. D., of Yale University, and the Reverends Samuel B. Sherrill and Stephen G. Hopkins, who have reviewed the present volume in manuscript.

C. F. K.

BERLIN, GERMANY,
January 2, 1897.

CONTENTS

PART I

THE PRE-ASSYRIAN PERIOD OF HEBREW HISTORY

I

THE HISTORICAL SOURCES FOR THE PERIOD

SECTIONS 1-12. PAGES 3-11.

SECTION 1. The general character of the sources. 2. The editor of the Book of Kings. 3. Ancient state records. 4. Analysis of I. Kings xii.-xvi. 5. The Elijah stories. 6. Historical value of Kings. 7. Characteristics of Chronicles. 8. Point of view of the chronicler. 9. His didactic purpose. 10. Sources of the chronicler. 11. Historical value of Chronicles. 12. Phœnician and Moabite inscriptions.

II

THE CHRONOLOGY OF THE TWO KINGDOMS

SECTIONS 13-17. PAGES 12-15.

SECTION 13. The chronological data of Kings. 14. Different chronological systems. 15. Exactness of Assyrian dates. 16. Synchronisms between Hebrew and Assyrian history. 17. Chronology of the Pre-Assyrian period.

III

THE DIVISION OF THE HEBREW KINGDOM

SECTIONS 18–26. PAGES 16–25.

SECTION 18. The causes of the division. 19. Early separation of Israel and Judah. 20. The division following the death of Saul. 21. Mutual jealousy under David. 22. Results of Solomon's policy. 23. Attitude of the prophets. 24. Orientalism *versus* Jehovahism. 25. Rehoboam's policy and its fruits. 26. Results of the division.

IV

RESOURCES AND ORGANIZATION OF THE TWO KINGDOMS

SECTIONS 27–34. PAGES 26–34.

SECTION 27. The boundary between Israel and Judah. 28. Their natural defences. 29. Their relative productiveness. 30. Elements of unity and discord. 31. Position of the king in the north and the south. 32. The national religion of Israel. 33. Northern sanctuaries. 34. Significance of Jeroboam's religious policy.

V

POLITICAL EVENTS IN ISRAEL AND JUDAH

SECTIONS 35–45. PAGES 35–45.

SECTION 35. The reigns of Jeroboam and Rehoboam. 36. War between Israel and Judah. 37. Accession of Omri. 38. His wars with Damascus. 39. The building of Samaria. 40. The policy of Ahab. 41. Aramean invasions. 42. Ahab's victory over the Arameans, and defeat at Karkar. 43. His death at Ramoth-Gilead. 44. Joram's unsuccessful invasion of Moab. 45. Contemporary events in Judah.

VI

THE RELIGIOUS CRISIS IN ISRAEL, AND THE WORK OF ELIJAH

SECTIONS 46–54. PAGES 46–54.

SECTION 46. The religious life of Judah. 47. Position of the prophets in the two kingdoms. 48. Results of Ahab's alliance with Phœnicia. 49. False and true Jehovah prophets. 50. The danger from Baalism. 51. Character of Elijah. 52. His protest against Baalism. 53. Ahab's crimes against his subjects. 54. Elijah's work as a social and religious reformer.

PART II

THE ASSYRIAN PERIOD OF ISRAEL'S HISTORY

I

THE HISTORICAL SOURCES AND CHRONOLOGY

SECTIONS 55–58. PAGES 57–60.

SECTION 55. The analysis of II. Kings iv.–xvii. 56. The prophecies of Amos and Hosea. 57. Assyrian inscriptions. 58. Chronology of the period.

II

THE REVOLUTION OF JEHU

SECTIONS 59–68. PAGES 61–69.

SECTION 59. The contrast between Elijah and Elisha. 60. The prophetic guilds. 61. Character of the "sons of the prophets." 62. Elisha's relation to the prophetic guilds. 63. The anointing of Jehu. 64. The murder of Joram. 65. Death of Jezebel. 66. Jehu's slaughter of the royal family. 67. The disastrous effects of the revolution. 68. Establishment of the principle of separation.

III

ISRAEL UNDER THE RULE OF THE HOUSE OF JEHU
SECTIONS 69-76. PAGES 70-77.

SECTION 69. Jehu's tribute to Assyria. 70. Damascus and Assyria. 71. Israel's subjection to Damascus. 72. Aramean invasion. 73. Unexpected deliverance. 74. Humiliation of Damascus by the Assyrians. 75. Extension of Israel's power. 76. Its Indian summer under Jeroboam II.

IV

THE PROPHETS AMOS AND HOSEA
SECTIONS 77-84. PAGES 78-85.

SECTION 77. The new type of prophets. 78. Their characteristics. 79. Nationality and position of Amos. 80. His call to be a prophet. 81. The reception of his message. 82. Personality of Hosea. 83. His private history. 84. Historical importance of these prophets.

V

SOCIETY AND MORALS IN ISRAEL
SECTIONS 85-90. PAGES 86-91.

SECTION 85. The causes of Israel's sudden decline. 86. Importance of the individual in the Hebrew state. 87. The results of the war with Damascus. 88. Increasing greed and luxury. 89. Public and private corruption. 90. Impending national destruction.

VI

POPULAR AND PROPHETIC RELIGION
SECTIONS 91-95. PAGES 92-97.

SECTION 91. The prevailing conceptions of Jehovah. 92. Corruption of the priests and prophets. 93. The God of Amos. 94. Sources of the new light. 95. Divine love as proclaimed by Hosea.

VII

THE DECLINE AND FALL OF ISRAEL

SECTIONS 96-102. PAGES 98-104.

SECTION 96. The reign of Menahem. 97. Conquests of Tiglath-Pileser III. 98. Parties in Israel. 99. Rebellion against Assyria. 100. Subjugation of Palestine by Tiglath-Pileser. 101. Intrigues of Egypt. 102. Revolt of Hoshea and the final fall of Samaria.

VIII

THE RÔLE OF ISRAEL IN THE WORLD'S HISTORY

SECTIONS 103-108. PAGES 105-110.

SECTION 103. The deportation of the Israelites. 104. Fate of the exiles. 105. Introduction of foreign colonists into Samaria. 106. Their religious faith. 107. Israel's literary products. 108. Its religious contributions.

PART III

THE ASSYRIAN PERIOD OF JUDAH'S HISTORY

I

THE HISTORICAL SOURCES AND CHRONOLOGY

SECTIONS 109-115. PAGES 113-119.

SECTION 109. The analysis of II. Kings xi.-xxi. 110. Date of Isaiah's prophecies. 111. Micah's sermons. 112. Contemporary Assyrian inscriptions. 113. Chronology of the period. 114. Date of Hezekiah's accession. 115. Data suggesting the year 725 B.C.

II

FROM ATHALIAH TO AHAZ

SECTIONS 116-125. PAGES 120-126.

SECTION 116. The revolution led by Jehoiada. 117. Rejection of Baalism. 118. Repair of the Temple. 119. Invasion of Hazael. 120. Accession of Amaziah. 121. Conquests in Edom. 122. Judah's humiliation by Israel. 123. Character of Azariah (Uzziah). 124. His foreign and home policy. 125. His war against Tiglath-Pileser III.

III

THE CRISIS OF 734 B.C.

SECTIONS 126-134. PAGES 127-133.

SECTION 126. The invasion of the Israelites and Arameans. 127. Character of Ahaz. 128. The youthful Isaiah. 129. His call to be a prophet. 130. His words of encouragement to Ahaz. 131. The mysterious sign. 132. Isaiah's political insight. 133. His appeal to the people. 134. Submission of Ahaz to Assyria.

IV

SOCIETY AND RELIGION IN JUDAH

SECTIONS 135-143. PAGES 134-140.

SECTION 135. The new influences in the life of Judah. 136. Social sermons of the prophets. 137. Oppression of the poor by the rich. 138. Results of intemperance. 139. Corruption of the rulers. 140. Earlier conceptions of Jehovah. 141. Popular superstitions. 142. False religious leaders. 143. Debasing ceremonials.

V

THE GREAT INVASION OF SENNACHERIB

SECTIONS 144–153. PAGES 141–150.

SECTION 144. The reign of Hezekiah. 145. Sargon's invasion of Palestine in 711 B. C. 146. Significance of the embassy of Merodach-Baladan. 147. Rebellion in Palestine. 148. Advance of Sennacherib. 149. Isaiah's predictions of Assyria's overthrow. 150. Conquest of Judah. 151. Surrender of Jerusalem. 152. Isaiah's activity at the great crisis. 153. Sennacherib's sudden retreat.

VI

THE WORK AND TEACHINGS OF ISAIAH

SECTIONS 154–163. PAGES 151–158.

SECTION 154. The greatness of Isaiah. 155. His conception of Jehovah's holiness. 156. His Messianic ideals. 157. His predictions concerning the Messianic king. 158. The coming Messianic kingdom. 159. The unfolding of the divine plan. 160. Growth of a prophetic party. 161. Doctrine of the "faithful remnant." 162. Reformation of Hezekiah. 163. The fruits of Isaiah's work.

VII

THE REACTIONARY REIGN OF MANASSEH

SECTIONS 164–169. PAGES 159–164.

SECTION 164. The causes of the religious reaction. 165. Triumph of the anti-prophetical party. 166. Introduction of foreign religions. 167. Work of Isaiah's disciples. 168. Editing of the Book of Deuteronomy. 169. Religious significance of the period.

PART IV

THE BABYLONIAN PERIOD OF JUDAH'S HISTORY

I

THE HISTORICAL SOURCES

SECTIONS 170-176. PAGES 167-171.

SECTION 170. The analysis of II. Kings xxii.-xxv. 171. The Book of Deuteronomy. 172. Prophecies of Zephaniah, Nahum, and Habakkuk. 173. Jeremiah's earlier sermons. 174. His later prophecies. 175. Ezekiel's earlier writings. 176. Babylonian and Greek records.

II

THE GREAT REFORMATION UNDER JOSIAH

SECTIONS 177-188. PAGES 172-182.

SECTION 177. The forerunners of the reformation. 178. Advance of the Scythians. 179. Zephaniah's reform sermons. 180. Call and character of Jeremiah. 181. Text of his earliest prophecies. 182. Finding of the book of the law. 183. Institution of reform measures. 184. Historical significance of the reformation. 185. The chief enactments of Deuteronomy. 186. Beginning of the rule of the written law. 187. Literary activity following the reformation. 188. Editing of earlier prophetical and wisdom books.

III

JUDAH AND THE NEW WORLD POWERS

SECTIONS 189-196. PAGES 183-189.

SECTION 189. The fall of Assyria. 190. Advance of Necho and death of Josiah. 191. The short reign of Jehoahaz. 192. Religious reaction under Jehoiakim. 193. Protests of Jeremiah. 194. Persecutions of the true Jehovah prophets. 195. Supremacy of the Chaldeans. 196. Counsels of Habakkuk and Jeremiah.

IV

JEREMIAH AND THE FALL OF JERUSALEM

SECTIONS 197-206. PAGES 190-198.

SECTION 197. The reception of Jeremiah's message. 198. His political policy. 199. His unflinching loyalty. 200. The first conquest of Jerusalem. 201. Inefficiency of Zedekiah. 202. Reappearance of old heathen forms. 203. Influence of the false prophets. 204. Revolt against Babylon. 205. Jeremiah's experiences during the siege of the city. 206. Final destruction of Jerusalem.

V

THE LAST CHAPTER OF JUDAH'S HISTORY

SECTIONS 207-212. PAGES 199-204.

SECTION 207. The Jewish colony at Mizpah. 208. Murder of Gedaliah. 209. Fortunes of the exiles. 210. Unique work and character of the Hebrew prophets. 211. Their constantly developing religious ideals. 212. Fulfilment of the prophetic revelation in Christianity.

APPENDIX 207-218

LIST OF MAPS AND CHART

CHRONOLOGICAL CHART	Frontispiece
THE TWO HEBREW KINGDOMS	to face page 26
THE ASSYRIAN EMPIRE	to face page 100

PART I

THE PRE-ASSYRIAN PERIOD OF HEBREW HISTORY

I

THE HISTORICAL SOURCES FOR THE PERIOD

1. THE glories of the united Hebrew kingdom attracted and held the attention of succeeding generations so effectually that the later prophets and priests whose writings are preserved in the Old Testament were impelled to draw copiously from the rich records which had been handed down from that earlier age. A period of decline, however, such as that which immediately followed the division of the kingdom, did not call forth the activity of the patriotic historian; neither were the events themselves of a character to appeal to religious teachers seeking for appropriate historical illustrations; consequently, our data respecting the Pre-Assyrian period of Hebrew history are at many points exceedingly incomplete.

2. The oldest and most authentic records are contained in I. Kings xii.–II. Kings iii. An examination of these chapters quickly demonstrates that, like the Books of Judges, Samuel, and I. Kings i.–xi., of which they are the continuation, they are compilations. As in the Book of Judges (I. sect. 32), the work of the editor or compiler is most apparent in the recurring formulas which constitute the framework into which the citations from the older sources are fitted. The

introductory formula in the case of the kings of Israel indicates the synchronism with the kingdom of Judah, and the length of the reigns of each king. In the case of the kings of Judah, the name of the queen-mother is also added, and frequently the age of the king at his accession. The closing formula consists of a reference to the historical source for the reign and to the death of the king, and usually gives the name of his successor. In the case of the kings of Judah, the words "was buried with his fathers" are added. The compiler's formula includes the stereotyped judgment upon each king. Even Zimri, who overthrew the house of Baasha and reigned in Tirzah but seven days, is condemned, as are all the kings of Israel who succeeded its founder, for "doing that which was evil in the sight of the Lord, in walking in the way of Jeroboam, and in his sin which he did, to make Israel to sin." A study of their recorded deeds indicates that the compiler commends or condemns them, not because of their ability or inefficiency as rulers, but according to their attitude toward the religion of Jehovah, and especially toward its ceremonial observances. His standard naturally was that of the later age in which he lived. The two kings who are accredited with "doing right in the eyes of the Lord" are Asa and Jehoshaphat, who instituted movements toward the reform of the religious cult.

3. These and kindred facts demonstrate conclusively that the interests of the editor of the Book of Kings were religious rather than political. This in turn explains why so many events of transcendent importance to the modern historian were either ignored or received only a passing notice. Fifteen times he refers

the reader for information respecting the acts of the different reigns to the "Book of the Chronicles of the Kings of Judah," and seventeen times to the corresponding Chronicles of Israel. These references — exceedingly tantalizing since there is no hope that the Chronicles can ever be recovered — suggest the sources from which he gained a part of his facts. Even though he lived after the final capture of Jerusalem, in 586 B. C., with which the narrative in Kings ends, it is not incredible that certain state annals were still accessible to him. The office of recorder, established under David (I. Kings iv. 3), is good evidence that some such memoranda of events were kept. The frequent change of rulers, especially in Israel, was, however, unfavorable for the preservation of a connected record. It is more probable that the Chronicles (literally, " words of days ") referred to were two independent, continuous narratives, based upon the official annals of the two kingdoms.

4. Chapter xii. 1–31 contains the account of the division of the kingdom, and the establishing of Jeroboam as king over Israel. The original source was probably the " Chronicles of the Kings of Israel," since the interest is with the north. In verses 26–31, the work of the compiler, who was strongly influenced by the ideas of the age of Josiah (sect. 188), is apparent. The language and representation of section xii. 32–xiii. 32, which tells of the mission of the unknown Judean man of God to the royal sanctuary at Bethel, indicate that it is a very late prophetic tradition, possibly inserted after the work of the compiler was completed. It has been suggested, not without reason, that it had its historical basis in the denunciatory mis-

sion of the Judean prophet Amos, to the royal sanctuary at Bethel, when another Jeroboam sat on the throne of Israel (sects. 79, 80). Verses 33 and 34 of chapter xiii. continue the thought of xii. 31, in the language of the editor. Chapter xiv. 1-18 consists of an ancient prophetic narrative, worked over in places by the same hand. The remainder of this chapter, and the two following, contain a series of short chronological and political notices cast in the framework of the compiler, broken only by the brief prophecy of Jehu against Baasha in xvi. 1-4.

5. The political notices are again interrupted by the insertion of chapters xvii.-xix. The thought and style of this section indicate that it is all from one source, which must have been an old prophetic history of the deeds of Elijah, based upon the stories current among the later prophets. Here the compiler has transcribed his material with few, if any, alterations. The abruptness of the beginning suggests that the original narrative was provided with an introduction, which he for some reason omitted. Chapter xxi. continues the Elijah history. In chapter xx., which breaks the continuity of the record, the interest is political, although in verses 35-43 the sons of the prophets are the central figures. It is evident that here, and in xxii. 1-38, the original source was Israelitish, and was also probably the prophetic records. The remainder of chapter xxii. consists of political notices incorporated in the regular framework of the compiler. The same are continued in II. Kings i. 17[b], 18. Between verses 1 and 17[b], however, is inserted a narrative concerning Elijah. Whether this is from the same source as the other Elijah stories or from a later

age, is uncertain. Chapter ii. concludes the history of Elijah, and introduces that of Elisha. In iii. 1–3 the familiar formula of the compiler reappears, while the remainder of the chapter, like I. Kings xx. and xxii., is in part political and in part prophetical, and was evidently drawn from an Israelitish source. The political notices of chapter viii. 16–29 conclude the treatment of this period.

6. This general analysis demonstrates that the different parts of Kings require careful study and adjustment by the historian. The testimony of the later traditions must be weighed in the light of their distance from the events of which they treat, and of the influences to which they have been subjected. The date and point of view of the compiler also must be constantly borne in mind. It may, however, be justly said that although the Books of Kings leave us ignorant of many important facts, they are, nevertheless, an exceedingly authentic historical source, since they are for the most part based upon records almost, if not quite, contemporary with the events recorded; and through them we are able to gain a remarkably clear conception of the essential movements of the period with which they are concerned.

7. While the second Book of Chronicles treats of the same epochs, its historical contributions are much inferior to those of the Books of Kings. In many passages the text is practically the same in each, indicating that the chronicler transferred bodily many sections from the older history. Consequently the Book of Chronicles is also a compilation; but only in a limited sense, for a study of the language and characteristics of the other parts of the book soon reveals

the fact that they are not citations from different sources, but are all from the same author, or, at least, from the same age and written from the same point of view.

8. His peculiarities are clearly marked. His use of words and constructions indicates that the Hebrew language was already beginning to decay. With the exception of one or two short notices, he completely ignores the history of Israel. He conceives of Judah as a religious state, very similar to the post-exilic hierarchy. He represents a ritual and institutions unknown to the pre-exilic historians, as already developed. Prophets are frequently introduced whose words and acts suggest no kinship with Elijah or Amos, but who are closely related to the legal prophets of the restored Jewish community. The evidence soon becomes conclusive that the author of Chronicles not only wrote long after the exile (the beginning of the Greek period, about 300 B. C., being the date usually assigned to him), but he also repeatedly read the ideas current in his age into the earlier days.

9. Two distinct strands, therefore, run through the book: the first consists of the citations from the Book of Kings; the second, of the writings of the chronicler himself. Although he has endeavored to reconcile them by omissions and expansions, the variations resulting from the two widely different points of view reflected therein are frequently apparent. The didactic aim of the chronicler is also very evident. National misfortune and prosperity are always attributed directly to right or wrong doing on the part of king or people. The attentive reader soon recognizes that the author has constantly in mind the Jews of his own day, whom

he was endeavoring in this manner to influence. The purpose which always dominated him, even more than the author of Kings, was to teach ethical and religious truth. With him the mere recording of historical facts was entirely secondary. If the systematic exaggeration of numbers which is found throughout the book is his work, it is the result, not of a deliberate effort to pervert the truth, but rather to make his illustrations the more impressive.

10. This preliminary study makes it possible to estimate approximately the historical value of the book. Since the citations from Kings only repeat what is known, additional information, if any, must be sought for in those parts of the book peculiar to the chronicler. Living as he did, centuries after the events recorded, the important question is, what were the sources, other than Kings, from which he drew his facts? He refers to (1) "The Book of the Kings of Judah and Israel" (II. Chron. xvi. 11, xxv. 26, xxviii. 26); (2) "The Book of the Kings of Israel and Judah" (II. Chron. xxvii. 7, xxxv. 27, xxxvi. 8); and (3) "The Acts of the Kings of Israel" (II. Chron. xxxiii. 18). These, probably, are to be identified as variations of the same title. In several cases facts not found in the canonical Book of Kings are cited from this "Book of the Kings of Israel and Judah," which is conclusive proof that they are not the same. It cannot be identified with the authorities referred to in the Book of Kings, since they were two independent works (sect. 3), treating the history of each kingdom separately. Reference is made in II. Chronicles xxiv. 27 to "The *Midrash* of the Book of Kings." *Midrash* (translated "commentary") is a late Hebrew designa-

tion for a treatise containing moral or religious teaching derived from some scriptural narrative or history. It is not impossible that this was still another title for "The Book of the Kings of Israel and Judah." If so, the chief authority of the chronicler was a post-exilic work, based upon the earlier traditions of the nation's history, written, like the Book of Chronicles, with the aim of deriving therefrom practical lessons for immediate application. The "words" of certain prophets and seers to which the chronicle refers may have been independent monographs, although the context suggests that they were only titles of certain sections of the greater work. Another source is called "The *Midrash* of the Prophet Iddo" (II. Chron. xiii. 22), suggesting that its character likewise was didactic rather than historical.

11. In the light of these facts there is no absolute proof that the chronicler had access to ancient sources equal or superior to those cited by the compiler of Kings. On the other hand, the representation of the chronicler is clear evidence that he drew his historical illustrations largely from current tradition. In many cases these differ radically from the testimony of the Book of Kings; for example, according to I. Kings xv. 1-4, Abijam, the successor of Rehoboam, "walked in all the sins of his father, which he had done before him; and his heart was not perfect with the Lord, his God," while the chronicler represents him (II. Chron. xiii. 1-22) as valiantly championing the cause of Jehovah, and winning a great victory over Jeroboam of Israel. This idealization of the history, in accordance with certain presuppositions current in the later days of the Jewish state, or as the result of long oral

EGYPTIAN AND MOABITE INSCRIPTIONS

transmission, runs through the entire book, and, of course, in many cases obscures the original kernel of historical fact. At the same time it is quite possible that certain details of the history have been preserved in this manner. When, however, the testimony of Kings and Chronicles differs, it is obvious that that of the older book is to be followed. Supplemental information contained in the Book of Chronicles must also be carefully weighed in the light of the tendencies of the author before being used.

12. Among the extra-biblical sources are the Phœnician inscriptions, which furnish valuable information respecting the religion of these neighbors of Israel. Later Hebrew and Greek writings have also preserved a few stray facts. The long inscription of Shishak I., inscribed in Egyptian hieroglyphics on the walls of the temple at Karnak, tells of his invasion of Palestine. The most valuable document, outside of the Bible, is the famous Moabite stone found east of the Jordan, and now preserved in the Louvre at Paris. This inscription consists of thirty-three lines, written in the so-called Phœnician script, on a monument of black basalt, reared by the Moabite king, Mesha, mentioned in II. Kings iii. 4, in commemoration of his victories over the Israelites. It refers to the conquest of Moab by Omri, and gives the details of the war with the Israelites, marvellously supplementing the biblical records.

II

THE CHRONOLOGY OF THE TWO KINGDOMS

13. HEBREW chronology presents a most difficult and perplexing problem. The biblical data respecting the chronology of the two kingdoms are of two kinds: (1) the length of each reign is given; (2) at the accession of each king the corresponding year of the reign of his contemporary in the other kingdom is stated. Addition of the years assigned to the kings of Israel and of Judah during a given period at once reveals differences which indicate that the first group of data is not exact. A comparison of the second, the synchronisms, with each other and with the lengths assigned to the different reigns, also discloses wide variations. These facts are not so surprising when it is noted that the chronological data belong, not to the citations from the older sources, but are from the hand of the compiler, who lived about the time of the fall of Jerusalem, in 586 B. C., and was therefore entirely dependent either upon earlier records or traditions for his information, or else, when these were wanting, was obliged to estimate as best he could. In the age of Jeremiah and Ezekiel it had become the custom to reckon time by the year of the reigning monarch, so that in the writings of these prophets he could find data from which to determine the length of each reign; but in the earlier periods there appears to have been no regular system of chronology, and no definite point from which to reckon. The older documents contain almost no chronological notices. Amos, the most exact of the earlier prophets, states that he delivered his prophecy "two years before the earthquake." Zechariah (xiv. 5) refers to the same great earthquake, which occurred during the reign of Uzziah of Judah; but succeeding generations soon forgot its exact date, so that the reference is now valueless.

14. The data upon which the compiler of Kings based his statements must have been exceedingly incomplete. "The Chronicles of the Kings of Israel and of Judah" may have given him the length of the reigns of certain kings, although the character of his system suggests that he was almost entirely dependent upon general tradition or his own estimates. A careful examination of the series of synchronisms confirms the conclusion that they were added by a still later editor, who was endeavoring to harmonize the differences in the chronology of the two kingdoms. A great variety of devices has been adopted by later biblical chronologists, with a view to explaining the discrepancies. That of Bishop Ussher, the one introduced in the margin of the Authorized Version, has in the past received the widest acceptance. The testimony of the Assyrian inscriptions, however, has demonstrated that his system can no longer be accepted as even approximately correct.

15. That which overthrows, at the same time furnishes the basis for a more satisfactory reconstruction. Fortunately the Assyrians, like the Greeks, designated

each year by the name of a certain officer. Not one, but many duplicate copies of these eponym lists have been found which mutually corroborate each other, and establish beyond question the exactness of the Assyrian chronological system. This is in turn carried down to later times by the Ptolemaic. Astronomical calculations have confirmed the testimony of these two systems respecting the month, as well as the year, when a certain great eclipse occurred. In accordance with the spirit of exactness, not only the length of the reigns of the kings, but also the events of each year, are clearly stated in the Assyrian annals and historical inscriptions. Consequently, when Hebrew and Assyrian history touch, an exact standard is provided for confirming or correcting the biblical data.

16. At two points the history of Judah and Israel absolutely synchronizes; namely, at the division, and when Jehu slew the rulers of both the kingdoms (sect. 64). The inscription of Shalmaneser II. states that Jehu paid tribute to Assyria in 842 B. C. Since there is no evidence that his territory was invaded, it is probable that his object in so doing was to establish his position on the throne of Israel; indeed, it would have been in perfect accord with the policy of Assyria if it had originally had a part in instigating the revolution. However that may be, 842 B. C. may be assigned as its date. Addition of the years attributed, respectively, to the kings who reigned between these two common dates, gives a total of ninety-five for Judah, and ninety-eight for Israel, which represents a difference of three years. The error should probably be assigned to Israel.

17. On an inscription of Shalmaneser II., Ahab of

CHRONOLOGY OF THE EARLIER PERIOD

Israel is mentioned among the allied kings who fought at Karkar in 854 B. C. (sect. 42). The battle of Ramoth-Gilead, at which Ahab met his death (sect. 43), was necessarily later, probably in the succeeding year, 853 B. C., eleven years before the revolution of Jehu. The biblical historian, however, assigns two years to Ahaziah, and twelve to Jehoram, the two kings who reigned between Ahab and Jehu. Ahaziah's fatal accident, recorded in II. Kings i. 2, probably came about the time of his accession. His brother Jehoram naturally became regent; in which case the two years of his regentship before Ahaziah's death would be counted twice. Since Ahab was living in 854, the duration of Jehoram's reign must have been eleven instead of twelve years. With these changes, the chronology of Judah and Israel is brought into agreement. According to this reckoning, the division of the Hebrew empire took place in 937 B. C., a date confirmed by the Egyptian monuments, since it falls within the reign of Shishak I., who received the refugee Jeroboam, and later invaded Palestine (sect. 35). These results, together with the contemporary chronology of Egypt, Damascus, and Assyria, are presented in the chronological chart at the beginning of this volume.

III

THE DIVISION OF THE HEBREW KINGDOM

18. WITHIN a single century the barbarous Hebrew peasants had been organized into a powerful empire which dominated the Canaanitish world. Still greater political influence and prosperity seemed to await them, when suddenly the empire was divided, and a few centuries later the two kingdoms, mutually weakened, fell an easy prey to foreign conquerors. What were the causes of this fatal act of division, so weighted with far-reaching consequences? A casual reader of Old Testament history might at once reply that it was due to the unwise course followed by Solomon's successor in his treatment of the northern tribes. This, however, would present only the immediate cause, — the spark which set off the accumulated mass of tinder. To understand the real causes, it is necessary to review the preceding chapters of Hebrew history.

19. When the fragmentary records of the Book of Judges at times turned the flash-light upon the Hebrew tribes contending for the possession of the soil of Canaan, or absorbing and assimilating the original inhabitants of the land, we found the Israelites, in the north and centre, and the Judeans in the south, each fighting their own battle alone, and each grappling

with their own individual problems (I. sects. 40, 41). Gideon's kingdom does not appear to have extended farther south than the limits of Ephraim. Nowhere is there any indication (in the light of the oldest sources) that during the period of the judges the north and south were ever united, even temporarily, to ward off the attack of a threatening enemy. Furthermore, a strong line of Canaanitish cities, of which Jebus was the chief, extended across the land of Canaan from east to west, completely cutting off the Israelites of the north from their kinsmen of the south. The Judeans also absorbed an unusually large native element, which undoubtedly tended to neutralize the mutual attraction of common blood and religion. Thus the circumstances and events of their early history all tended to foster the spirit of independence rather than of union. The frequent recurrence, side by side, in the earlier as well as in the later narratives of Samuel and Kings, of the two names Israel and Judah as designations of the north and south, respectively, indicates that this distinction was constantly maintained, even during the period of the united kingdom (I. Sam. xi. 8; xvii. 52; II. Sam. xi. 11; xii. 8; xxi. 2; I. Kings i. 35; iv. 20, 25). In the oldest sections in Judges the same distinctions are observed (i. 2, 4, 8, 28; v. 2, 3, 5, 7, 8, 9, 11, etc.). Not until after the fall of the northern kingdom does Israel, as a general name, appear to have been also applied to Judah. This looser usage is most common in Chronicles. In this connection it may be noted that the tribes in the north after the division were assuming no new title when they designated their kingdom as Israel.

20. Under the stress of a common and threatening danger (subjection to the Philistine yoke), all the tribes were driven for a brief period to unite about the standard of the Benjaminite Saul. If the support of the Judeans was at first strong and hearty, it was gradually withdrawn when their kinsman and popular champion, David, was hunted from the court of their suspicious king. Although they did not openly revolt, the readiness with which they proceeded, after the battle of Gilboa, to elect their favorite to the throne of Judah, even though the northern tribes remained faithful to the house of Saul, shows conclusively that their support of the Benjaminite king was far from enthusiastic, and that the feeling of jealousy was only smouldering.

21. Throughout all early Hebrew history the northern tribes, of which Ephraim and Manasseh were the acknowledged leaders, far surpassed Judah in influence and resources. Joshua, Deborah, Barak, Gideon, Samuel, and Saul, whose exploits were the pride of the race, all came from the north; but the scion of the house of Saul, whom the Israelites placed upon the throne after the death of their first king, proved a weak reed to lean upon; while from without the victorious Philistines pressed them so severely that their might was terribly broken. At last the stroke of assassins cut down in quick succession both their general and their king, so that they were left without a leader. Under the pressure of this insistent danger, the Hebrew tribes were for the first time in their history really united. David's continued success in war, and a policy which favored the northern tribes even more than Judah, preserved the union; neverthe-

less during his reign the ancient, fierce rivalry broke forth and threatened to sunder the state. In his efforts to conciliate the northern tribes after the suppression of the rebellion of Absalom, David unwittingly stirred up the jealousy of the Judeans. Evidently, while endeavoring to appease them, he in turn incensed their old rivals of the north; for we find them in a mad revolt, which is only put down by Joab by force of arms. This incident is conclusive proof that the old bitter feeling survived, and that all the skill and power of a David was required to keep together the elements which mingled so imperfectly.

22. Solomon took good care, at the beginning of his reign, to remove by the sword all persons who might prove seditious. Perhaps he felt too secure after this act, since his later policy is famous for just those mistakes which his father had so carefully avoided. He succeeded in realizing his ideal of splendor and absolutism; but his success was purchased at a terrible cost. Although for a time his people were dazzled by the display, erelong the northern tribes waked up to the bitter realization of the fact that all this glitter was not gold, and that the just policy of David no longer guided the throne. Israelitish interests were made subservient to those of the king and of Judah. It was gall and bitterness to the northerners to see the wealth and power of the empire constantly being concentrated in the southern capital. Furthermore, the Temple and all the splendid palaces and strong fortifications with which the city was beautified were built by the fruits of their increase and by their wearisome toil. Thus to

override the rights of the individual subject and to reduce to serfdom a people who a generation before had been free and independent, inevitably meant rebellion whenever opportunity offered. Many may have been the uprisings. History records only the unsuccessful one led by Jeroboam the Ephraimite.

23. In connection with the account of this rebellion, there is a suggestive notice (I. Kings xi. 29-39) to the effect that Jeroboam was informed by a prophet, Ahijah, that he would become king over the ten tribes. Even though the narrative be late, it is of value as indicating the hostile attitude of the prophets toward the policy and reign of Solomon. This is further confirmed by the reference, in I. Kings xii. 22-24, to the action of a certain man of God, named Shemaiah. When Rehoboam, after the division, gathered together his forces to march against the Israelites to reduce them to subjection, this man of God appeared before the king, and proclaimed that it was the will of Jehovah that they should not go up and fight against their brethren. The narrative also adds that the Judeans listened to him and desisted from their expedition. These references are sufficient to indicate that the influence of at least the more zealous Jehovah-prophets was thrown on the side of the Israelites, and that they favored rather than opposed the division. The attitude of the true prophets in subsequent crises, when conditions were similar, confirms the conclusion.

24. A careful study, on the one hand, of the reign of Solomon and of the tendencies which were then beginning to manifest themselves, and, on the other, of the character and ideals of these early men of God, reveals the cause of their attitude. Solomon's policy

brought to the Hebrew nation the refining influences and the products of the civilization of that ancient world. Through the newly opened channels of conquest and commerce it was fast absorbing the art and ideas of the surrounding peoples. In a generation or two more it would have been quite impossible to distinguish it from its neighbors. If its character and mission were to be similar to that of the other nations of the world, this transformation certainly represented great progress; but if it had a peculiar mission, and if that mission could be performed only as it preserved a unique individuality, this was not an altogether promising line of development. Also, according to the fundamental principles of a Semitic alliance, Solomon was obliged to acknowledge the gods of the allied peoples, and to tolerate their worship within the territory of Israel. The crisis was more than a political one; it was also religious. It was Solomon's policy of Orientalism versus the pure worship of Jehovah. The future of the faith of humanity hung in the balances. Probably the prophets did not fully appreciate the stupendous issues at stake, but they saw enough to lead them to act. They were ready to welcome the disunion of the tribes as the last resort, in the hope that thereby they might avert the awful danger which threatened the faith which they held dearer than the unity of their nation. Hence, before Rehoboam mounted the throne of his father, the circumstances of their early history, the bitter jealousy between the north and the south, and the injustice and grinding oppression of Solomon, which had aroused the uncompromising opposition of the prophets as well as the resentment of the proud tribes of the north, had prepared the way for the division.

25. A king with the commanding prestige and tact of David might have averted the catastrophe for a time. But Rehoboam, reared in the luxurious Oriental court of Solomon, possessed neither of these qualities. The laws also which determined the right of succession in Israel evidently had not as yet been definitely established. Saul and David had been chosen by the nation to be their leaders and counsellors. Solomon had been nominated as his successor by the aged David, and this had been publicly ratified — at least, by the citizens of Jerusalem. Hence it appears that the Hebrew people had thus far had an important voice in the election of their king, although the tendency to regard the office as hereditary was beginning to manifest itself. The northern tribes, discontented with the heavy burdens and unjust partiality of Solomon's rule, had good precedents as well as reasons for refusing to accept Solomon's son as their king until they were given certain assurances that these evils would be abated. Accordingly they meet at the old northern capital, Shechem, whither Rehoboam, apparently attended by only a small force, goes to confer with them. The demand which they make is reasonable : " Lighten the grievous burdens which your father laid upon us." It is probable that if the king had yielded, the dismemberment of the empire might even then have been averted. Ostensibly he acknowledges its justice, for he half consents in asking for three days for consideration. Graphically, the author of Kings presents the counsels of the different factions in Rehoboam's camp. The gray-bearded courtiers, who had been instructed by the politic David, and who had grown old in the service of the worldly-wise Solomon, appreciate the situation and

THE ACT OF DIVISION

urge a conciliatory policy — at least, until the present crisis is past. But the younger men, who, like himself, had grown up in the vitiated court of Solomon, had only absorbed its ideas of Oriental absolutism. Naturally he accepts their advice, since it merely voices his wishes. Despotism shall win or lose the day. Therefore, at the end of the appointed time, when the representatives of the northern tribes again assemble, confidently expecting a generous Magna Charta, a bomb is exploded in their midst. " Whereas my father did lade you with a heavy yoke, I will add to your yoke; my father chastised you with whips, but I will chastise you with scorpions," are the arrogant words of the king. It instantly kindles into a fierce blaze all the suppressed jealousy and discontent which filled their hearts. The old cry of revolt, raised during the days of David by Sheba the Benjaminite (II. Sam. xx. 1), "What portion have we in David? To your tents, O Israel," spreads like wild-fire from mouth to mouth throughout the assembly. The aged Adoram, who was at the head of the hated levy, is sent to treat with the Israelites, and falls the first victim of Rehoboam's folly. It is forever too late for conciliation. The die is cast. Before Rehoboam has reached Jerusalem, whither he had fled for his life, king of but one tribe, Jeroboam, who in the earlier days had led the revolt against the tyranny of Solomon, and had now returned from his forced exile in Egypt, had been raised to the throne of Israel. The Judeans, who naturally refused to accept the choice of the majority of the tribes, are regarded as rebels by their kinsmen of the north. The old breach was opened too widely ever to be closed again.

26. The act of division turned the future course of Hebrew history into entirely new channels. Its effects can be clearly traced in all the varying fortunes which subsequently came to the Hebrew race. It is idle to conjecture what might have been, had the integrity of the empire been preserved; but it is certain that the division sapped the political strength of the Hebrew people, so that the possibility of their becoming a great world-power was forever destroyed. With few exceptions their subsequent history is one of continuous political disaster. On the other hand, the mighty tide of foreign customs and civilization which came in during the reigns of David and Solomon was turned suddenly backward. The energies of the people were occupied in a death-struggle for national existence. Consequently, for a few generations at least, the social life tended necessarily to return to its primitive simplicity. The influence of Solomon's policy of exalting the court far above the mass of the nation was arrested, and thereby greater equality among all classes was secured. The tendency to place Jehovah on an equality with the gods of the surrounding nations was also temporarily checked. The series of political calamities which soon overtook Israel, and later Judah, called forth those religious heroes, the prophets, who won mighty victories for righteousness and Jehovah. When the northern kingdom fell in 722 B. C., Judah, severed from it by the division, survived to enjoy a century of independent existence, which was rich in spiritual experience. By virtue of its separation, its religious life was centralized more and more in Jerusalem, thereby preparing the way for that centralization of worship which in time became one of the

strongest bulwarks against the influence of heathenism. The approaching captivity, which followed in the wake of the division, led the prophets to open their spiritual eyes wider until they beheld, instead of the local god of one little nation, a Lord supreme in the affairs of men and in the universe. Out of the depths of their private and national affliction, those divinely enlightened men caught glimpses of the character and will of the Eternal, which enabled them to rise above national annihilation and exile, and to give to their race and humanity truths and principles which are the everlasting foundations of religious faith. Thus, while by the division the Hebrew nation lost its life, in a truer and higher sense it found it.

IV

RESOURCES AND ORGANIZATION OF THE TWO KINGDOMS

27. THE territory of the two kingdoms which came into existence as the result of the division, was defined by tribal rather than natural boundaries. The border line between them lay within the land of Benjamin, and the greater part of the territory of this tribe must have fallen to the northern kingdom. The Benjaminites regarded themselves as belonging to the house of Joseph (II. Sam. xix. 16, 20). Their traditions and the events of their earlier history all bound them most closely to the tribes of the north. They had every reason to regard with no kindly interest the family of David, which had supplanted that of their kinsman Saul. Their resentment, in fact, found repeated expression at the time of Absalom's rebellion during the lifetime of David, and almost resulted in the dismemberment of the kingdom (II. Sam. xvi. 1-14; xx. 1-22). Consequently, there is every reason for accepting the testimony of I. Kings xii. 20, which states explicitly, "There was none that followed the house of David, but the tribe of Judah only," instead of the popular impression that Benjamin joined with the south. The boundary line must have run a few miles north of Jerusalem, including within the limits

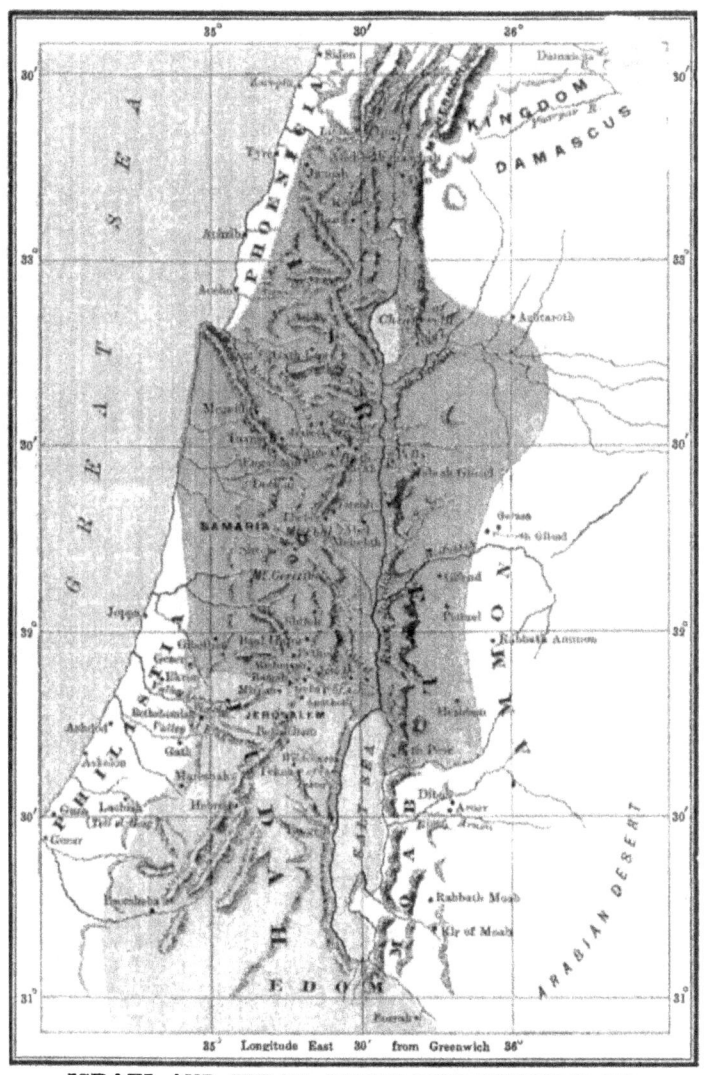

ISRAEL AND JUDAH AFTER THE DIVISION OF THE HEBREW EMPIRE.

of Judah a small section of the territory of Benjamin immediately adjacent to the southern capital. It varied at different times, and proved a fertile subject of dispute (I. Kings xv. 17-22). During the reign of Asa, Ramah (about six miles north of Jerusalem) was fortified by the Israelites. When the forces of the north were withdrawn, the Judeans improved the opportunity to fortify in turn the neighboring towns of Geba and Mizpah (five miles north of Jerusalem). The Judean territory probably never extended beyond these points.

28. The area of the territory of the southern kingdom could not have been more than one-half of that of its northern rival, while the amount of arable land was less than one-fourth. The area of Judah, however, during the greater part of its history was greatly increased by the territory of Edom, over which the Judeans continued to exercise a suzerainty. Similarly, at the division, the territory of the Moabites fell to the tribes of the north. Although the land of Judah was much smaller, it enjoyed certain advantages of position not shared by the northern kingdom. On the east, the Dead Sea, with its barren shores, proved an efficient barrier against Moabite or Ammonite invasion. On the south extended the desert, which barred the way against all invaders, except the wandering Arabs, whose attacks, although troublesome, were no menace to the nation's life. After their power was broken by David, the Philistines, whose lands bounded Judah on the west, never again united for the conquest of Hebrew soil. For two centuries the northern kingdom proved an effective buttress against the formidable attacks of the great world powers from the north.

The only foe which Judah had cause to fear was Egypt, and Egypt's ambitions and capabilities were limited to desultory forays into Canaan. Israel, on the other hand, by virtue of its position was obliged to engage in a constant and desperate struggle for existence. Its bars were all down. The broad valleys which led into the heart of the land furnished natural highways for hostile armies. Egyptian invasion penetrated its territory also, while from the northeast there came, almost yearly, Aramean, and later Assyrian armies, which gradually drained its life-blood.

29. The natural resources of the two kingdoms presented even greater contrasts. Judah's territory was strewn with limestone rocks. The little soil between yielded only a meagre subsistence in return for the most wearisome labor. Water, the absolute requisite for animal and vegetable life, was doled out by nature most sparingly. While great wealth was impossible, a sufficient livelihood could be gained by toil. It was a land calculated to develop hardy, earnest, courageous men, fond of their rocky hills, and tenacious of their customs and religion. It furnished no surplus of products to tempt its inhabitants to seek a foreign market, and the barriers which encircled them intensified the tendency to remain at home. In Israel, on the contrary, the rocks were concealed by rich soil, abounding in springs which called forth everywhere a rich vegetation. Broad plains, easily tilled, furnished a generous supply of grain. Contrasted with Judah, it was indeed "a land flowing with milk and honey." Its wealth, however, encouraged commerce and attracted the invader. It gave to Israel material prosperity and commanding prestige, but with these came temptations

and dangers unknown to Judah. It tended to develop a luxurious, pleasure-loving people, far more susceptible to foreign influences than their poor cousins living among the limestone hills in the south.

30. Judah's inferiority in size and numbers was more than compensated for by the unity and homogeneity of its population. The tribe of Judah not only dominated the southern kingdom, but it had so completely absorbed the Simeonites, and the Arabian clans, which it had found in possession of its southern territory, that it was a nation made up of one tribe. The interests of the people were the same, since their land presented little diversity and limited its inhabitants to the culture of the vine and the raising of sheep and cattle. Jerusalem towered so high above the few other towns in the kingdom that they stood toward her only in a relation of dependence. In this respect Judah resembled states like Damascus, Babylon, and Rome. Furthermore, the Temple, with its splendid equipment, commanded the reverence and homage of all the people, and was, therefore, a potent uniting force. These elements of strength and union were lacking in Israel. Ephraim, the leading tribe, shared its influence with others. Rival sectional interests were an even greater source of weakness. The tribes in the extreme north and across the Jordan never participated actively in the common national life of Israel. Natural divisions, like the plain of Esdraelon and the deep valley of the Jordan, kept the different sections of the northern kingdom from coming into close touch with each other. An inevitable result of the wide variations in physical contour was that its inhabitants were found engaged in a great

variety of occupations. In the territory of Ephraim and Manasseh, for example, agricultural and pastoral pursuits flourished side by side; on the rich plain of Esdraelon the life was wholly agricultural; in the north, fishing as well as the culture of the soil occupied the people; while across the Jordan the majority of the inhabitants were shepherds. Consequently, while Judah was a perfect social unit, bound together by the closest natural bonds, Israel was made up of a loose aggregation of such units. In the north also there was no capital city like Jerusalem, nor sanctuary like that reared by Solomon, dominating and binding together all these different elements, which from geographical, racial, and political causes were so heterogeneous.

31. Furthermore, in Israel, where a strong central government was most needed, it was most conspicuously lacking. In Judah the kingship was hereditary, and was retained in the same family throughout its history, so that its rulers enjoyed the prestige of the name of David, and all the cumulative power which comes from an uninterrupted succession. The priesthood, which exercised great influence, used this to maintain the authority of the throne, by which it was in turn supported. The prophets also co-operated with the civil rulers to further the political interests of the nation. Throughout Judean history the relations of court and people were most cordial. Therefore the authority of the king was practically absolute without being tyrannical. In Israel these conditions were in many respects reversed. Jeroboam I. was raised to the throne from the ranks of the people. His authority, therefore, was delegated, and he enjoyed none of the

prestige of a long established royal line. His influence, like that of the judges of earlier days, and the kings who succeeded him, depended chiefly upon his own personal ability. When an Israelitish king was weak or incapable, his authority was little more than that of his most powerful nobles. This fact explains why so often in the northern kingdom an aspiring subject was able to mount the throne by the assassination of his sovereign. These frequent revolutions tended still further to weaken the authority of the central government. Consequently, the strength of Israel was constantly being sapped, not only by foes from without, but by inefficient rule and anarchy within.

32. Jeroboam I. felt impelled, as the first king of a newly constituted kingdom, to establish a royal sanctuary which should be closely identified with the new *régime*, and enjoy in a peculiar sense the kingly patronage. Late historians, who lived when all the ceremonial worship had been centralized in Jerusalem, regarded this act as in itself a sin; but it is clear, in the light of subsequent history, that at this time even the Judeans worshipped at many shrines outside of Jerusalem, and that Jeroboam did not thereby discountenance the other sanctuaries, like Gilgal, Shiloh, and Mizpah, already established in the territory of Israel (Amos iv. 4; Hosea v. 1; I. Sam. i. 3, 9). In reality he was only acting in accordance with the precedent established by Gideon (I. sect. 55) and Solomon (I. sect. 154), and performing his duty as the religious as well as civil head of the nation. Instead, however, of following minutely the example of his predecessors and establishing a new shrine at his capital, he selected, doubtless with a view to securing

the support of the priests, two sanctuaries, located conveniently for his people, and indicated that they were to be the royal shrines by setting up at each a calf or bull, probably made of wood overlaid with gold. The bull seems to have been regarded among the Hebrews and other Semitic peoples as a symbol of majesty and strength (compare Deut. xxxiii. 17). It appeared in the supports of the brazen sea of Solomon's Temple, probably in the horns of the altar, and possibly in the form of the cherubim which guarded the Ark of Jehovah. Colossi, with the body of bulls, are also familiar figures before every ancient Assyrian palace. That the Israelites originally regarded them as symbols of Jehovah can scarcely be questioned; indeed, the author of Kings explicitly states that Jeroboam identified them with the god who delivered the Israelites from Egypt (I. Kings xii. 28).

33. From such zealous prophets as Elijah and Elisha this act of Jeroboam's evoked no censure; in fact, it must have been regarded as eminently satisfactory by the conservatives of his realm, for instead of establishing a new shrine, hallowed by no traditions from antiquity, he merely assumed the attitude of patron toward two of the most venerated and popular sanctuaries in the land. The one at Dan, in the north, had been established during the period of the judges, and was presided over by the family of a certain Levite of Bethlehem, who traced descent from Moses (I. sect. 69). Bethel, as its name ("House of El") signifies, was regarded as a sacred city by the Israelites, at least since the time of its capture. According to Judges xviii. 30, the same priestly family continued in charge of the sanctuary of Dan

from the days of the judges to the captivity. If it was necessary for Jeroboam to appoint new priests to meet the additional requirements of the services at the sanctuary in Bethel, which seems to have enjoyed in a greater measure the royal patronage, he could refer, as a precedent, to a similar appointment by David (I. sect. 123). The ritual at these shrines probably did not differ materially from the one at Jerusalem during the same period. The author of Kings recalls the fact that the great annual feast in Israel was held in the eighth month instead of the seventh, as was the custom in Judah in his time. It may also be inferred that on this occasion the king, like Solomon before him (I. sect. 162), publicly sacrificed at the great altar in Bethel. The prophet Amos, a few generations later, refers to the custom of going up to Bethel and bringing sacrifice every morning, and tithes every three days, and of offering sacrifices of thanksgiving of that which is leavened, and of proclaiming free-will offerings (iv. 4, 5). He also speaks of the solemn assemblies and public sacrifices in terms which suggest that they were attended with song and music, and even with licentious practices (v. 21–24; ii. 8).

34. Although his contemporaries did not recognize it, the policy which Jeroboam adopted in regard to the national religion was a hindrance to the development of the purer worship of Jehovah. About the sanctuaries which he thus exalted, clung all the debasing traditions and customs of a less enlightened past The golden bulls also belonged to the degrading symbolism of the preceding age. His act, therefore, represented a step backward rather than forward. Later

prophets, who recognized the evils which followed in its train, were right in branding it as a fatal mistake. Keeping alive dead traditions and forms, because they had served the past well enough, instead of adopting a higher expression of truth, was the sin "wherewith Jeroboam, the son of Nebat, made Israel to sin." In this respect the newly established temple at Jerusalem, untrammelled by few inherited traditions, enjoyed advantages which were destined ultimately to make it a centre of commanding influence.

V

POLITICAL EVENTS IN ISRAEL AND JUDAH

35. THE dissolution of the empire of David precipitated a long series of petty wars between the different peoples of the Palestinian world. In the contest between Israel and Judah the advantages at first were with the smaller kingdom, since it inherited most of the collected wealth of the empire. Rehoboam, who evinced the same incapacity for war that had characterized his father, did not, however, improve his opportunity, but contented himself with establishing fortresses throughout the territory of Judah. Jeroboam in the meantime fortified his capital, Shechem. Located in a narrow valley commanded by Gerizim on the south, and Ebal on the north, it could never be made an impregnable stronghold. The author of Kings states that he subsequently "went out from thence and built Penuel," which is to be identified with the east-Jordan town south of the Jabbok, upon which Gideon at an earlier period wreaked such dire vengeance (I. sect. 54). Later Tirzah, which was probably located about six miles northeast of Shechem, became the capital of the northern kingdom (I. Kings xiv. 17; xv. 33). The superiority which Judah at first enjoyed disappeared a few years later, when

its territory was invaded by Shishak, the Lybian commander who founded the twenty-second Egyptian dynasty. Jerusalem was captured, and the wealth which David and Solomon had collected was transferred to Egypt. Within Judah bronze henceforth took the place of gold in the court as well as in the Temple. According to the inscription which Shishak caused to be inscribed on the south wall of the great temple of Amen at Karnak, commemorating this plundering expedition, Israel suffered together with Judah; for several of the one hundred and thirty-three captured cities mentioned therein belonged to the north.

36. When this wave of invasion had receded, the war between the two Hebrew kingdoms was renewed. After a reign of twenty-two years Jeroboam died and was succeeded by his son Nadab, who was assassinated soon after his accession by a certain Baasha of the tribe of Issachar, while he was besieging the Philistine town of Gibbethon. According to the chronicler, Abijam, the son of Rehoboam, gained an important victory over Jeroboam. Baasha, the new king of Israel, however, carried on the war with fresh vigor. Ramah, on the extreme southern border of Israel, was fortified, and the independence of Judah was so threatened that its king, Asa, in alarm, collecting the gold and silver which he could find in his court and the Temple, sent them as a present to persuade Benhadad, the king of the new Aramean state which had been founded at Damascus by Rezon during the reign of Solomon (I. sect. 143), to break his treaty with Baasha. Benhadad, ambitious for conquest, responded by invading the territory of Israel, capturing the cities of Dan, Abel, and Ijon in the north, and overrunning the land

around the Sea of Galilee. Baasha was obliged to withdraw his forces from the south, and Asa improved the opportunity to fortify Geba and Mizpah. The Judean king by this act secured immediate deliverance, but he thereby introduced into Israelitish politics a foe who was destined for generations to harass and menace both the Hebrew kingdoms.

37. Elah, the son who succeeded Baasha, proved an even more inefficient ruler than the son of Jeroboam. In a drunken debauch he was slain by Zimri, one of his military officers. In accordance with the custom of the age, his family were exterminated by the same hand. The assassin sat but seven days on the throne thus rendered vacant. As soon as the news of this deed reached the army engaged in the siege of Gibbethon, they at once elected their general, Omri, king, and marched against the conspirator, who remained at the capital, Tirzah. When Zimri realized that resistance was useless, he retired to the palace and burnt it down over his head. During this period of anarchy another party in Israel set up as king a certain Tibni, the son of Ginath. In the civil war which followed, Omri was ultimately successful, and became the founder of the strongest dynasty which occupied the throne of Israel.

38. Fortunately for the existence of Israel, Omri proved an able and energetic military commander; for Benhadad of Damascus, its northern foe, was strong and pressing it closely. The record in Kings preserves none of the details of the wars between Damascus and Israel, which were fought during the twelve years of Omri's rule. On the whole, they must have been adverse to the northern kingdom; for Ahab,

Omri's successor, was little better than a vassal of Benhadad during the earlier part of his reign (I. Kings xx.). An incidental reference informs us that Omri ceded certain Israelitish cities to his foe, and that he was also compelled to set aside certain streets in his capital — probably for the especial use of Aramean traders — which were under the especial patronage of the king of Damascus (I. Kings xx. 34). In that age this act was one of the penalties imposed by the conqueror upon the vanquished. In the east his military enterprises were attended with greater success; according to the testimony of the Moabite stone, "Omri was king of Israel and oppressed Moab many days, for Chemosh was angry with his land" (lines 4–6).

39. Under his wise direction the relations between Israel and Judah became more and more friendly, until in the days of Ahab the two Hebrew kingdoms are found fighting together against their common foes. The most important act of his reign, however, was the establishment of Samaria as the capital of his kingdom. Since the latter days of Jeroboam the kings of Israel had resided at the insignificant town of Tirzah. Omri purchased for two talents of silver a commanding hill, situated a few miles northwest of the ancient capital, Shechem, surrounded on every side by deep valleys, and encircled by some of the most fruitful territory in all Israel. On this site, centrally located and capable of being easily rendered almost impregnable, he built Samaria, which was thus identified with his family, and which subsequently figured so prominently in Israelitish history. Although he never attained as great success, since the conditions were much more unfavor-

ble, Omri from a political point of view stands in much the same relation to Israel as David did to the united Hebrew kingdom. The Assyrians, even when Jehu had supplanted the family of Omri, recognized his ability by designating Israel as "the House of Omri."

40. Ahab, his son, adopted the policy of Solomon, although he evinced far more energy as a military leader than that splendor-loving monarch. At Samaria he engaged in extensive building operations, while at Jezreel, on the edge of the fair plain of Esdraelon, he had another palace. During his reign the prevalent spirit of building impelled Hiel, the Bethelite, to rebuild Jericho (I. Kings xvi. 33, 34). Under the rule of the preceding dynasties, Israel had had no relations with the surrounding nations except those imposed by war. Omri or else his son, who succeeded to his ambitions, recognizing the material advantages which would accrue to Israel, surrounded as it was by so many hostile peoples, from an alliance with the opulent trading city of Tyre, renewed the old relations which had existed during the days of David and Solomon, and cemented them by a marriage between Ahab and the daughter of the Tyrian king.

41. The author of Kings gives few suggestions respecting the sequence of events in Ahab's reign; this question, therefore, must be determined from a study of the events themselves. His father had been obliged to make important concessions to Benhadad of Damascus. The greater part, if not all, of the territory of Israel north of the plain of Esdraelon and east of the Jordan, had been seized by this powerful foe. Ahab submitted to his demands until at length the Aramean

king assembled all his forces and invaded Israel for the purpose of completely subjugating it. He succeeded in overrunning its territory and in shutting up the king of Israel within his capital Samaria. Ahab at first acceded to Benhadad's demand that he become his vassal. Not content with this concession, the Aramean king insisted that the city and palace be given up to his servants for plunder. Ahab recognized that he could hope for no leniency. Accordingly, after consulting with his elders and people, he sent back a refusal, which called forth from Benhadad dire threats of vengeance. Ahab retorted in the words of the proverb, "Let not him that girdeth on his armor boast himself as he that putteth it off," and forthwith mustered his army for an attack, although his entire fighting force was less than eight thousand. At midday they fell upon the Arameans, while Benhadad was engaged in a drinking-bout with his princes. When it was reported to the reveller that the Israelites were approaching, he gave the senseless command to take them alive. In a short time his army was in flight, and he himself was fleeing for his life.

42. His counsellors consoled the vanquished king with the assurance that his defeat was because the god of the Israelites was a god of the hills, and that on the plains he could expect a victory. They also wisely suggested that he substitute military commanders for the inefficient princes. Acting in accordance with their advice, Benhadad invaded Israel in the following year with a great army to meet with a still more overwhelming defeat at Aphek, which may have been the Aphek memorable in the Philistine wars (I. sect. 59), but more probably is to be identified with the modern

town of Fîk, located five miles east of the Sea of Galilee, and therefore in the direction from which the Arameans would naturally advance. He himself was unable to escape, but was compelled in the garb of a suppliant to crave mercy from the king of Israel. Although the prophets of his realm severely denounced Ahab for his leniency, he spared the life of his foe, and allowed him to depart on the condition that he would restore the Israelitish cities captured from Omri, and set aside for the Israelites certain quarters in Damascus. Ahab's motive in so doing can only be conjectured. Possibly it was because he recognized in the approach of Assyria a common adversary which demanded their united attention. The fact that these hereditary foes did actually fight side by side with the other princes of Palestine against Assyria at Karkar in the year 854 B. C. is established by the testimony of the inscription of the Assyrian king, Shalmaneser II. The land of Damascus is accredited with furnishing twelve hundred chariots, twelve hundred cavalry, and twenty thousand soldiers, while Ahab, of the land of Israel, sent two thousand chariots and ten thousand soldiers. The only satisfactory explanation of how Ahab, whose territory was not especially adapted for chariots, was able to furnish more than his rich northern rival, is that the battle of Karkar followed soon after the great Israelitish victory at Aphek.

43. Shalmaneser claims that he completely routed the forces of the Palestinian coalition. He did not, however, immediately follow up the results of his victory, being recalled by more important affairs in the east. Thus Damascus and Israel were free to resume their old attitude of hostility. After about a year of

peace Ahab again took up the gauntlet. The cause was that the king of Damascus had failed to restore the Israelitish cities, as promised at the treaty of Aphek, for the attack was directed against Ramoth-Gilead, showing that it was still retained by the enemy. Jehoshaphat of Judah, lured by the false message of the four hundred servile prophets of Israel, joined the campaign. Ahab, knowing that he himself was an especial object of hate to the king of Damascus, entered the battle in disguise. A chance arrow, however, pierced through his armor and inflicted a mortal wound, so that at evening he died. The army, thus bereft of a leader, gave up the fight and scattered, each man to his home.

44. The death of Ahab was the beginning of a long series of disasters for Israel. Ahaziah, who followed him, fell through a lattice in the upper chamber of his palace at Samaria, and received injuries from which he never recovered. He and his brother Joram, or Jehoram, who succeeded him, carried on the policy of their father, but with little of his military ability. Mesha, the shepherd king of Moab, improved this opportunity to throw off completely the yoke of Israel. Joram summoned his father's ally, Jehoshaphat of Judah, and his vassal prince, the king of Edom, with their armies, to aid him in subduing the rebel. Instead of invading the territory of Moab from the north, where it was most easily defended, they took the longer and more difficult route around the southern end of the Dead Sea, where they almost perished for lack of water. The Moabites, attacked in their rear, were put to flight and their territory devastated. The Moabite king was shut up within his capital, and, after making

a vain effort to escape with some of his followers, resorted to the extreme measure of offering up his oldest son on the walls, as a burnt-offering to appease and thereby win the favor and aid of his god. The act is quite in keeping with the religious practices of the age, and with the spirit which finds expression in the Moabite inscription. It aroused the superstitious fear of the allies, and proved the signal for their retreat. Moab was thus lost to Israel; while in the north the contest with Damascus, which at this time was weakened by the attacks of the Assyrians, was carried on without marked success on either side. At last the religious storm which had long been gathering within Israel broke, in the revolution of Jehu, sweeping the family of Omri from the throne, and inaugurating another era in the history of the northern kingdom.

45. According to the testimony of Chronicles (II. Chron. xiv.), during the reign of Asa, Judah was invaded by an Egyptian army, led by Zerah, who is probably to be identified with Osorkon II. The Judean king, collecting his forces, met and defeated the marauding foe at Mareshah, near the Philistine border. Jehoshaphat, the son of Asa, who was the first to enter into friendly relations with Israel, was an energetic and aspiring prince. Although his warlike ventures in connection with the northern kingdom were universally unsuccessful, he infused new life and activity into Judah. Garrisons were placed in the walled towns, citadels and store-cities built at strategic points, and the army regularly organized (II. Chron. xvii.). In the south he carried his conquests to the Red Sea, and forced certain of the wild, desert tribes to pay him a

large annual tribute. Imitating Solomon, he prepared to send from the port of Ezion-geber large merchant-ships to Ophir. These, however, were wrecked even before they had left their port. Under his son, Jehoram, Judah met with still further reverses. The town of Libnah successfully revolted. In the campaign against the Edomites, who at the same time renounced the yoke of Judah and "made a king over themselves," Jehoram with his army barely escaped from being surrounded and captured, by cutting his way by night through the line of the insurgents. The alliance between Israel and Judah was cemented by the marriage of Jehoram to Athaliah, one of the daughters of Ahab. The court of Judah imitated more and more that of Israel. Ahaziah, who succeeded to the throne of Judah, joined his cousin Joram in his war against the Arameans, and fell a victim to the destroying zeal of the reformer Jehu. Athaliah, the queen mother, seized this opportunity, by the murder of the seed royal, to assume the supreme power. For six years Judah endured her tyranny, until a wave of revolution headed by Jehoiada, the priest, cut down the usurper and placed upon the throne of Judah, Jehoash, the youthful son of Ahaziah, who had been rescued by his aunt from the massacre instituted by Athaliah. From a political point of view the Pre-Assyrian period of Hebrew history was one of steady decline, only temporarily checked by the energetic efforts of such kings as Jehoshaphat, Omri, and Ahab. The rich resources of Israel were being exhausted by repeated revolutions; the strength of the Hebrew race was being wasted by a fruitless civil war; and the energies of the entire Palestinian world were being dissipated by internecine conflicts waged with the cruelty and destructiveness characteristic of the age. Before Assyria, which was destined radically to transform the character of Palestinian politics, appeared on the horizon, conditions in Canaan were ripe for its conquest.

VI

THE RELIGIOUS CRISIS IN ISRAEL, AND THE WORK OF ELIJAH

46. THE data are too incomplete and unsatisfactory to determine with certainty what was the character of the religious life of Judah during the century immediately following the division. Under Rehoboam and Abijam, the religious conditions introduced by Solomon's policy continued unchanged. The reigns of Asa and Jehoshaphat were, however, characterized by renewed political and commercial activity, and with this came certain movements toward religious reform which served to extend the influence of the Temple and of its priesthood. The most odious symbols of Baalism were removed, and its most immoral practices suppressed; but the author of Kings, as well as later conditions, testifies that, "nevertheless the high places were not taken away; the people still sacrificed and burnt incense in the high places" (I. Kings xxii. 43). Inasmuch as Jehoshaphat's spirit of reform did not deter him from readily affiliating with the house of Omri, which openly tolerated Baalism, and from listening as willingly to the prophets of Israel as to those of his own land, it must be concluded that religious ideas and practices in the south were not radically better than those in the north.

INFLUENCE OF THE PROPHETS IN ISRAEL 47

47. In religion, as in politics, Israel played the leading rôle. In both kingdoms, the priests of the sanctuaries were conservative rather than progressive religious forces, cherishing existing customs and loyally supporting the ruling monarchs. Upon the prophets, therefore, devolved the high duty of delivering their nation from the grave dangers which threatened, and of leading it on to a higher and purer religious life. The author of Kings refers incidentally to one or two prophets in Judah, and the chronicler to still others; but there is no evidence that they exerted much influence. In Israel, however, the conditions were entirely different. The prophets favored the division (sect. 19), because they hoped in the new kingdom to be able to realize their ideals. Their hopes were partially fulfilled. Freedom from the dominating authority of the throne was temporarily secured, and much of the old simplicity restored; but it was a reversion to the conditions which obtained during the days of the judges. The foreign wars and the dangers of national annihilation soon called forth a series of military kings, who had no sympathy nor concern for the realization of the lofty religious ideals which filled the souls of the greatest prophets. Consequently, between the monarchy and prophecy, the two leading powers in Israel, there was an intense and ever-growing opposition. It first found expression in messages of denunciation and warning, directed by the prophets against the reigning sovereigns (I. Kings xiv. 1–17; xvi. 1–4).

48. The antagonism between prophet and king reached its culmination in the persons of Elijah and Ahab, who were each the strongest representatives of

the two opposite tendencies. The causes of the conflict were the same as those which earlier led to the division of the Hebrew empire. Ahab, as we have seen (sect. 40), was, like Solomon, intent only upon making Israel a strong political power, and upon establishing his own authority. The means which he used were well adapted to his ends. The newly founded towns of Samaria and Jezreel grew into cities, adorned with public buildings. The currents of commerce were set in motion through an alliance with Tyre. New ambitions filled the minds of the rude shepherds and farmers as they came into contact with foreign life and civilization. With Phœnician wares and customs came, inevitably, Phœnician religion. Ahab was bound to countenance it by the obligations of his alliance. In Jezebel, the daughter of Ethbaal, the ex-priest of Baal, who had mounted the throne of Tyre by murdering his predecessor, Phœnician culture found a champion as ardent as she was unprincipled. Ahab sealed the alliance, and gratified his queen by building at Samaria a temple and altar of Baal. This called for special priests, who enjoyed Jezebel's patronage. Ahab and his political advisers indignantly resented the charge of committing any sin against Jehovah in thus recognizing the god of an allied people. Even if the king did at times pay his respects at the sanctuary of Baal, he had no intention of abandoning the worship of the god of his nation. Perhaps the best evidence of this is that to his children, Ahaziah, Jehoram, and Athaliah, he gave names which contained the shorter form of Jehovah (Jah or -iah), the designation of their god peculiar to the Hebrews.

49. From a political point of view, Ahab's general

FALSE AND TRUE PROPHETS

policy, although calculated to alter fundamentally the character of Israel, appeared to be wise and beneficial. It was only the more enlightened prophets, representing the best conscience of the nation, who recognized the menace which it was to the pure worship of Jehovah. Those who had dared to raise their voices in protest had been silenced, and in some cases persecuted; for Ahab regarded them as mere fanatics, blind to the best interests of Israel, and rebels defying his authority. Jezebel recognized in them the most zealous opponents of her policy. According to the narrative preserved in I. Kings xviii., she personally undertook to exterminate these "troublers of Israel." Their cause was also betrayed by the many in Israel who were called prophets of Jehovah, and who, nevertheless, prophesied only according to the dictates of self-interest. This fact is vividly portrayed in the picture contained in I. Kings xxii. Jehoshaphat of Judah and Ahab of Israel are about to go out in battle against the Arameans at Ramoth-Gilead, when, in accordance with the prevailing custom, the Judean king makes the demand, "Inquire, I pray thee, at the word of the Lord to-day" (verse 5). In compliance, Ahab summons four hundred (a general number) of the prophets of Jehovah. Unanimously they predict, "Go up; for the Lord shall deliver it [Ramoth-Gilead] into the hand of the king." Jehoshaphat, suspecting their subserviency, asks whether there is no other prophet from whom he may inquire. Ahab replies reluctantly that there is a certain Micaiah, the son of Imlah, whom he hates because he always prophesies evil. While awaiting his arrival, the four hundred prophets reiterate their prediction of victory. To impress it, one of them makes horns of iron and declares, "Thus saith Jehovah, with these shalt thou push the Arameans until they be consumed." The royal messenger, who summons Micaiah, urges him to return a message agreeable to the king; but he replies, "What Jehovah saith unto me, that will I speak." Mockingly he repeats before the kings the words of the four hundred prophets. When Ahab adjures him to speak the truth, he proclaims, in the figurative language of prophecy, "I saw all Israel scattered upon the mountains, as sheep that have no shepherd." Then, by the use of an allegory, he tactfully but forcibly declares that the message of the other prophets is false, being prompted by a lying spirit. His fidelity is repaid by the blows of his fellow prophets, and painful imprisonment at the command of the king.

50. The scene belongs to the last days of Ahab's life, and is conclusive evidence that he never ceased to regard Jehovah as the god of Israel. The real danger was more insidious, for it was that the distinctions between the religion of Jehovah and Baal would be completely levelled. The incident just referred to indicates that at least the majority of the official prophets of Jehovah abetted rather than opposed this tendency. The ceremonial forms with which Jehovah and Baal were worshipped were so similar that the priests could maintain no essential distinctions. The cultivation of the soil was the chief industry of Israel; and Baal was pre-eminently the god of agriculture, while Jehovah had from the first been associated with the nomadic life of the desert. To understand the gravity of the situation, it is necessary to remember how attractive to a Semite of that age was the religion

of Baal, which gave the greatest license to its devotees. Its system of morals was the antithesis of that preached by the austere prophets of Jehovah. Gradually and almost imperceptibly, Israel was again becoming politically, socially, and religiously like the other nations about, — a consummation fatal to the performance of its unique mission to the world.

51. One man alone had the courage to act. Later generations, appreciating something of the sublimity of Elijah's personality, cast about it an atmosphere of wonder. Ahab and many of his contemporaries regarded him as an arch-fanatic. From the biblical narrative we learn that his home was among the hills east of the Jordan, on the borders of the desert in that part of the land which retained longest the customs and thought peculiar to nomadic life. He was, therefore, in sympathy with those who regarded with apprehension Israel's departure from the ancient pastoral simplicity. It was a feeling which found objective expression in the vow of the Nazirite not to touch the product of the vine, since this was regarded as the characteristic symbol of Canaanitish agricultural civilization; and in the customs of the Rechabites, who also refused to drink wine and clung persistently to their nomadic life (Jer. xxxv.; II. Kings x. 15–23). In mode of living and thought, Elijah always retained the characteristics of a "sojourner in Gilead." His religion also was that of the desert, which had been the cradle of the Mosaic faith. He was unaffected by the seductive spell of the Canaanitish civilization, and had little sympathy with the current aspirations for material wealth and political glory. His one ideal was that Israel should be in the true sense the people of Jeho-

vah. Toleration of the worship of Baal was to his enlightened vision entirely incompatible with the realization of that ideal. It must, therefore, be suppressed, even though at the cost of the nation's existence.

52. The method which he employed to accomplish this was characteristic of the man. Ahab had no inclination, even if he had had the ability, to understand and fulfil his demands. Accordingly he appealed from the king to the people. Famine, which was always recognized as a sign of Jehovah's displeasure, first did its work of preparation. It is interesting to note in the same connection that Meander of Ephesus also refers to a drought during the reign of Ethobalos (Phœnician, Ethbaal), King of Tyre, which lasted one year and was finally averted, according to Phœnician tradition, by the intercession of the king. According to the narrative in Kings, at Elijah's command, to which Ahab was forced to defer, the people assembled on Mount Carmel. On its heights popular superstition and the religion of Jehovah met face to face, and the weakness of the one and the strength and grandeur of the other were manifest. Upon the minds of the people was flashed anew and with unparalleled clearness the old truth, so nearly forgotten, that Jehovah is a jealous God, and that therefore they must make an absolute choice between him and Baal. Not only his words and acts, but also the personality and manner of the great prophet-hero impressed the lesson. Baal was vanquished, and his priests, who were present, were slain; the cause of Elijah's God for the moment triumphed; but at the close of that memorable day the people returned to their homes, and Jezebel

practically retained her old power. Nothing seemed to have been gained. Truth is not impressed upon humanity by the tempest, nor by the lightning-flash, nor in a moment, but gradually. Teachers were needed to move among the people and inculcate the great truth by word and life. Elijah must have realized his utter inability to complete the task which he had undertaken. He had done all that he could, and much more was needed. With supreme fidelity to human nature, tradition records the despair which in the moment of reaction filled his impulsive, heroic soul.

53. Elijah was not only the herald of a purer conception and a truer service of Jehovah, but he also proved himself the champion of the rights of the people against the aggressions of the throne. Ahab's policy of absolutism manifested itself in his palace building and the suppression of the prophets who challenged his authority. It found its most heinous expression, however, in an incident recorded in I. Kings xxi. Near the royal palace at Jezreel was the vineyard of a peasant by the name of Naboth. The king, desiring to extend his grounds, endeavored to secure it by purchase; but the Jezreelite, availing himself of the right of every free citizen of Israel, refused to part with his family possession. Ahab returned to his palace in a pet. Jezebel, familiar only with the methods of an Oriental monarch, taunted him because he had stopped to regard the rights of his subject, and despatched letters to the elders of Jezreel, commanding them to bring against Naboth the charge of blasphemy, and forthwith to stone him to death. The queen evidently knew her instruments, for the crime was speedily committed. When Ahab went

down to take possession of the vineyard so iniquitously gained, Elijah met him with a bitter denunciation on his lips, and the proclamation that because of this deed destruction would come upon himself and family.

54. The horror which this royal crime aroused in the minds of the people undoubtedly did more to overthrow the house of Omri than the favor shown to the Phœnician Baal; for they felt, with reason, that the hereditary rights, of which they were always exceedingly jealous, were thereby endangered. Notwithstanding the distinguished services of the house of Omri, popular discontent against it continued to grow, and was reinforced by the opposition of the Jehovah prophets until it found expression in the bloody revolution of Jehu. Undoubtedly this revolution was one of the indirect fruits of Elijah's work, but his contributions to Israel's development were positive as well as negative. He does not appear to have brought forward any new revelation, but by word, and especially by his life, he impressed upon his age the simple yet revolutionizing truth that Jehovah, the god of their race, was a jealous and righteous God. Being jealous, he accepts nothing less than the entire service of his people. Being righteous, he demands righteousness in turn from his followers. The heroic prophet of Jehovah left the scene of his struggles before the principles for which he offered himself gained general acceptance; but he left behind him a personal ideal of simple grandeur, of undaunted courage, and of unswerving advocacy of the demands of divine righteousness, which was partially realized in the prophets who followed him, and only fully in the second Elijah, who heralded the coming of the One altogether righteous.

PART II

THE ASSYRIAN PERIOD OF ISRAEL'S HISTORY

I

THE HISTORICAL SOURCES, AND CHRONOLOGY

55. THE story of the gradual decadence and final destruction of Israel is recounted in II. Kings iv.–xvii., in a series of citations from various sources. The first part of the section (iv. 1–viii. 15; xiii. 14–21) consists of stories concerning Elisha. Variations in language and context indicate that they are not all from the same hand (compare verses 23 and 24 of chapter vi.; also v. 27, and viii. 4, 5). Chapters iv., vi. 1–7, and viii. 1–6 manifest the closest affinity with one another. All the Elisha passages, however, are characterized by the same picturesqueness of style, the same general point of view, and the same indications of the influence of oral transmission as the Elijah narratives (sect. 4), and hence were doubtless current in the same prophetic circles in Israel during the ninth and eighth centuries B. C. The compiler has introduced them into his history with very few changes. The material in chapters ix. 1–x. 27, which records the revolution of Jehu, although taken from several different sources, is evidently old. It is closely related to the politico-prophetical material contained in I. Kings xx., xxii., and II. Kings iii. The remaining passages, which refer primarily to Israel, are, with the exception of

the short section xiv. 8-14, epitomes from the hand of the compiler. In chapter xvii. 7-23 he reviews the causes which in his opinion led to the fall of the northern kingdom, and in verses 24-41 explains the origin of the Samaritan people and of their religion.

56. Our conception of this period would be very defective if we were dependent alone upon the fragmentary records of Kings. Fortunately portions of the sermons of two prophets who prophesied in Israel have been preserved. These are the most valuable historical sources, because they represent the testimony, not only of eyewitnesses, but of the most enlightened men of their age. Through their eyes we are able to study conditions as they actually existed, and to become familiar with the details of the history. The prophecy of Amos deals especially with the social questions which agitated Israel during the days of Jeroboam II. It is a perfect unit, the parts being closely related, and, with the exception of a few possible interpolations, is all from the hand of the prophet himself. The prophecy of Hosea, who lived a few years later, is, on the contrary, exceedingly disconnected. The repetitions of theme and ideas and the loose correlations of the parts indicate that it is based upon extracts from different sermons. It is sharply divided into two parts. The first includes chapters i.-iii. The reference in i. 4 to the house of Jehu as still standing is conclusive evidence that the section belongs to the latter days of the brilliant reign of Jeroboam II. In the second part, chapters iv.-xiv., the historical background is entirely different. Anarchy has succeeded the order of the earlier days; there are several references to the murder of a king

(vii. 3-7, 16; x. 15); Israel has lost her prestige (vii. 8; viii. 8), and is foolishly seeking alliances with Egypt and Assyria, in the hope that it can secure help from them (v. 13; vii. 11; viii. 9; xii. 1). Evidently most of the sermons from which these were taken belong to the days of disorder and decline which followed the death of Jeroboam II., antedating, however, the invasion of Tiglath-Pileser in 734 B. C., when Gilead was wrested from Israel (vi. 8; xii. 11).

57. The historical inscriptions of the great Assyrian conquerors, Shalmaneser II., Tiglath-Pileser III., Shalmaneser IV., and Sargon, who extended their campaigns into Palestine, furnish many facts supplemental to the biblical data. Through them the student is introduced to the broader field of Semitic politics, and enabled to study those movements of which the Hebrew kingdoms were the victims. Although the Assyrian annalists frequently exaggerate, and sometimes suppress unpleasant facts, this tendency is easily detected. Their testimony is of inestimable value, since it is that of writers living at the time that the events transpired. The exact chronological system which they contain has revolutionized our conclusions respecting the chronology of this period.

58. The Assyrian inscriptions establish the date of the fall of Samaria at 722 B. C. Beginning in 842 B. C., the Assyrian period of Israelitish history was, therefore, limited to one hundred and twenty-one years. The total number of years assigned in the biblical narratives to the kings of Israel from Jehu to the fall of Samaria is one hundred and forty-three, presenting a discrepancy of twenty-two years. Here again the Assyrian inscriptions suggest where the error is to be

found. In 738 B. C. Menahem paid tribute to Assyria. This date also gives approximately the year of his accession, since the biblical account definitely states that Israel's king gave the Assyrian king one thousand talents, "that his hand might be with him to confirm the kingdom in his hand" (II. Kings xv. 19). The total number of years assigned by the compiler to the kings who reigned in Israel during the seventeen years between 738 and 722 B. C. is forty-one (ten, two, twenty, and nine). Evidently the twenty-two extra years have been inserted here. Four years later, 734 B. C., Tiglath-Pileser invaded Israel, putting to death Pekah who had cut down Pekahiah, the son of Menahem. These facts indicate that the round numbers (ten and twenty) assigned to Menahem and Pekah, are greatly exaggerated. Menahem may have reigned three, while Pekah's rule could not have exceeded two years. On the other hand, the nine years attributed to Hoshea, and the one hundred and three to the house of Jehu, are confirmed, giving as the result a comparatively definite system (see chart).

II

THE REVOLUTION OF JEHU

59. ALTHOUGH the principles which Elijah valiantly advocated did not gain immediate recognition with court and people, he did succeed in impressing them indelibly upon the minds of certain of his followers. Chief among these was Elisha. According to I. Kings xix. 16-21, he was from the town of Abel-Meholah, which was situated on the southern side of the plain of Bethshean, not far from the Jordan. His home, therefore, was in the midst of a rich agricultural community, and his father, Shaphat, was one of the rich farmers of Israel. His call to the prophetic office was unprecedented, for he is the only prophet who, according to the biblical record, was summoned to that high calling by another. At first his relations to Elijah were those of a disciple and servant (II. Kings iii. 11). A more striking contrast could not be imagined than existed between the rugged, fearless prophet of Gilead and his follower. The one represented the uncompromising life and religion of the nomad, while the other belonged to the agricultural class in Israel and was familiar with the customs of city and court. The stories respecting these two prophets which were current in the prophetic schools during the succeeding centuries, illustrate how different was the impression which the two men made upon posterity. With the name of Elijah was associated the drought, the thunder-roll, and the lightning-flash, — wonders within the realm of Nature. Elisha, on the other hand, was always found among men, healing their maladies, cleansing their fountains, and advising king and subject. The one used denunciations to accomplish his ends, the other diplomacy; in the eyes of his contemporaries the one seemed to fail, the other to be crowned with complete success; and yet Elijah will always be recognized as the master, the greater soul who dared to initiate.

60. At this critical point in Israelitish history the prophetic guilds (I. sect. 86), which were mentioned first during the days of Samuel, again come into prominence. They were located at the larger cities, like Jericho (II. Kings ii. 5), and especially at the old sanctuaries, such as Bethel (II. Kings ii. 3) and Gilgal (II. Kings iv. 38). Their members stood in much the same relation to the religion of Jehovah as the prophets of Baal to the Phœnician cult (I. Kings xviii. 19, 22). They were permitted to marry, and entered into business contracts with their fellow countrymen (II. Kings iv. 1). Certain of them, at least, lived together, as at Gilgal, sharing a common table (II. Kings iv. 38-41). These guilds sometimes changed their place of abode, and built their quarters with their own hands (II. Kings vi. 1-7). They must have been dependent for their subsistence chiefly upon their own toil, although they may have received some support from the throne, as did the priests of the royal sanctuaries and the prophets of Baal, who enjoyed the patronage of Jeze-

NATURE OF THE PROPHETIC GUILDS   63

bel. The subserviency of the four hundred Jehovah prophets, who were summoned before Ahab and Jehoshaphat (sect. 45), indicates that they must have anticipated some material reward. This incident also suggests what were the functions of the members of these prophetic guilds. Questions, private as well as public, concerning which it was deemed necessary to consult Jehovah, were referred to them. According to Deuteronomy xviii. 9–15, the prophets filled the place in Hebrew life left vacant by the diviners, wizards, and necromancers to which the people were accustomed to resort in the earlier days. Their services, therefore, would call forth private donations. In II Kings v. 22, Gehazi, the servant of Elisha, is represented as soliciting a gift in behalf of two young men of the sons of the prophets, who had recently come from the hill country of Ephraim.

61. There is no direct information respecting the manner in which the members of these prophetic guilds were chosen. The term "son of the prophets" is used, not to indicate lineal descent, but in the common Semitic sense of the member of a community. Personal inclination or natural characteristics undoubtedly had much to do in determining the choice. The account of the call of Elisha (sect. 59), and the references to his servant, Gehazi, suggest that the older prophets gathered about themselves young men, who attended them and, as an inevitable result of association on such terms, absorbed much of their spirit and teaching. A group of such followers would easily grow into a guild. The application to these bands of the modern term "school," with its implication of regular instruction, is not warranted by any biblical reference, and is en-

tirely out of harmony with the habits of the Orient. Undoubtedly much of the old frenzy and wild enthusiasm characterized their religious life. The son of the prophets who anointed Jehu was called a mad fellow by the other officers in command of the Israelitish army (II. Kings ix. 11, 12); even Elisha employed a minstrel to induce that ecstatic state which they deemed essential for prophesying.

62. While they shared certain external characteristics, the Hebrew prophets differed widely in their teachings. The four hundred who predicted victory for Ahab (I. Kings xxii.) must have come from the various prophetic guilds; and yet there was no sympathy between them, and Micaiah, the son of Imlah, or the unknown son of the prophets who declared that judgment would surely come upon Ahab because he spared the life of Benhadad (I. Kings xx. 35-43). Instead, the reference indicates that already there were two distinct classes of prophets in Israel: the true prophets, like Elijah and Micaiah, who saw clearly the will of Jehovah and acted accordingly; and the so-called false prophets, who likewise prophesied in the name of Jehovah, but who had no divinely given message. It was this latter class which subsequently undermined the influence of the true prophets by destroying all confidence in the prophetic word. Among the more faithful sons of the prophets, Elijah's message to Israel must have met with the readiest response. As in the days of Samuel, they proved a political as well as a religious force. Elijah's successor, Elisha, assisted them in their building operations, helped them in adversity, and stood toward them in the relation of patron (II. Kings vi. 1-7; iv. 1-7, 38-41; v. 22). In them

he found in turn that support which was absolutely necessary if Baalism was to be overthrown.

63. For more than a decade after the death of Ahab, his family continued undisturbed on the throne of Israel. The author of Kings declares that Joram made a movement toward reform by "putting away the pillar of Baal which his father had made," but there was no essential change in the religious policy of the nation. Baalism was still openly tolerated, and Jezebel exercised her old influence. Meantime the resentment of the people, kindled by the injustice against Naboth, and the zeal of the prophets, jealous for Jehovah, increased until it was ready to burst into a fierce flame. Elisha was the one who applied the torch. On a certain day about 842 B. C., when the Israelitish army were carrying on the war with the Arameans, intrenched at Ramoth-Gilead, he called one of the sons of the prophets, and despatched him on a secret mission to the army. Joram, the king, had returned to Jezreel wounded, and so the messenger on his arrival was ushered into the presence of the captains of the host. Disregarding the rest, he addressed himself directly to one of them, a certain Jehu, saying, "I have an errand to thee, O Captain." As soon as the two were alone the prophetic messenger, in accordance with Elisha's command, poured the oil, with which he was provided, on Jehu's head, declaring that Jehovah had anointed him king over Israel, and immediately fled. The spirit of rebellion was in the air, and the act was so full of significance that when Jehu rejoined his fellow officers they inquired at once the reason of the strange visit of this fanatic. At first he attempted to turn them off, but they refused to be deceived. Then in his blunt

fashion Jehu announced that he had been anointed king. The details of the narrative suggest that this was only the launching of a conspiracy previously arranged. Conditions certainly were ripe. Stripping off their outer garments, his fellow officers cast them down upon the steps beneath Jehu's feet, and with trumpet-blast proclaimed him king.

64. Elisha made no mistake in the choice of a man to overthrow the house of Omri. Energy and craftiness were in him, combined with a certain recklessness, which has found popular expression in the saying, "He drives like Jehu." Impetuous, fearless, regardless of life, he was fitted alike to lead a cavalry charge or a dangerous revolution. He had also listened to Elijah as he pronounced the awful curse upon the house of Ahab, so that he regarded the reigning family as doomed, and himself as a messenger sent by Jehovah to execute his judgment. His ambition and fanaticism needed no further encouragement. Leaving the officers and army behind, with strict injunctions that no one should be allowed to bear the news of the conspiracy to the court, he himself set out in hot haste across the Jordan and up over the plain of Jezreel, which leads to the northern capital. When Joram, the wounded king, learned from the watchman that a company was approaching, he despatched a horseman to meet them, to learn whether their mission was a peaceful one. Jehu, grimly commanding the messenger to fall behind, rode on furiously. A second horseman was sent out with the same result. Soon he was near enough for the watchman on the battlements of the palace to perceive from his driving that it was Jehu. Recognizing that he came on important busi-

ness and not suspecting a conspiracy, the king set out to meet him, accompanied by Ahaziah, his cousin, the king of Judah, who was visiting him at the time. Jehu's reply to his salutation led him to fear treachery. As he turned to flee with Ahaziah he fell to the bottom of his chariot, pierced through the heart by an arrow from Jehu's bow. In remembrance of Elijah's prophecy against Ahab (sect. 53), the revolutionist commanded his faithful follower, Bidkar, to cast the body upon the land secured by foul means from Naboth the Jezreelite.

65. Jehu's fierce zeal against the house of Ahab led him to pursue the fleeing king of Judah across the plain of Esdraelon, and to command his followers to slay him. Near Ibleam Ahaziah received a mortal wound, from which he died at the famous old fortress of Megiddo. Jezebel was the next victim of Jehu's destructive hate. Attiring herself in all her finery, she met him with the taunting words, "Is it well, thou Zimri, thy master's murderer?" Without replying, he commanded the eunuchs in attendance to throw her down through the window. The order was immediately executed, and the fierce conspirator drove his chariot horses over her body. When he at last gave orders to his servants to bury the aged queen, it was found that the dogs had further fulfilled the prophecy of Elijah, and devoured the body.

66. Having exterminated the representatives of the reigning family at Jezreel, Jehu next turned to Samaria, where were seventy of the descendants of the hated Ahab. To the elders of the city and the guardians of the young princes he sent an ironical letter, suggesting that they elect one of their royal wards king and

defend him if they could. It awakened the response anticipated. In terror they submitted, and expressed their readiness to do whatever Jehu should command. He forthwith demanded the heads of the princes. When these were received at Jezreel, he caused them to be piled up at the city gate, as a gory proof of the complicity of the elders of Samaria in this wholesale slaughter. Forty-two of the princes of the royal house of Judah, whom Jehu overtook near Samaria, were mercilessly put to death. His thirst for blood was not satisfied until the nobles, favorites, and priests of Ahab were all slain. According to the narrative preserved in II. Kings x. 17-28, a large number of the followers of Baal shared the same fate.

67. By this revolution the house of Omri was completely exterminated, and the danger that Baalism would gradually supplant the worship of Jehovah forever averted; but at a terrible cost. The blood, so ruthlessly shed at this time, weakened Israel to such an extent that for the next half-century it was forced to maintain an almost hopeless struggle for existence. Even though the evil was great, it hardly justified the means employed to remove it. Either Elisha and the prophets who chose him were deceived as to the character of Jehu, or else had not yet learned that the cause of truth is not permanently advanced by intrigue and bloodshed. Amos and Hosea, looking back from the vantage-point of the next century, condemned this revolution, declaring, in the name of Jehovah, "I will visit the blood of Jezreel upon the house of Jehu" (Hosea i. 4; Amos vii. 9). The sword, thus fanatically unsheathed in the name of religion, was destined to be repeatedly used by friends and foes of Jehovah

with the same deplorable effects. Jehu proved himself to be little more than an unscrupulous adventurer who improved a favorable opportunity to further his own interests. From him the cause of the pure worship of Jehovah could expect little real assistance. He rooted out Baalism, but in its place he only restored the half-heathenish bull worship of Jeroboam.

68. At the same time this great prophetic revolution established a principle, enunciated in the earlier days and potent at the division of the Hebrew empire (sect. 26), which determined to a great extent the character of the history of Judah as well as Israel. It was that for which Elijah contended: "If Jehovah be God, follow him." Practically interpreted, this meant that under no conditions should the god of a foreign nation be recognized within the land of Jehovah; hence alliances between Israel and other peoples were forever impossible. Thus at this time was virtually instituted that complete separation, so jealously guarded by prophets, and later by priests, which made the Hebrews a holy (in its original sense of "separate") nation, and which appears even to-day in the sharp line of demarcation drawn between the Jew and the Gentile.

III

ISRAEL UNDER THE RULE OF THE HOUSE OF JEHU

69. THE bloody waves of revolution which about the middle of the ninth century B. C. swept in quick succession over the two Hebrew kingdoms, also affected Damascus. Even before Jehu raised his hand against the house of Omri, Hazael improved the opportunity, afforded by the illness of his master, the aged warrior, Benhadad II., to mount the throne by murdering him. Although Damascus was beset by strong and active foes, the usurper succeeded, by his energy and military powers, in raising it to a more commanding position than it had enjoyed under his predecessor. Jehu of Israel, however, possessed little of the ability of his northern rival, whose example he had imitated. The blood which he so freely shed in establishing his undisputed sway was that of the military class who had rallied about Ahab. Israel was divided into antagonistic parties, and the prophetic conservatives who had supported him had little interest in war. The biblical historian passes over the events of his reign with a brevity which is ominous. We are not surprised, therefore, to learn from the inscriptions of the Assyrian conqueror, Shalmaneser II., that he received the tribute of "Jehu, son of Omri," together

with that of Tyre and Sidon. On the Black Obelisk also the ambassadors of Jehu are pictured bearing gifts of silver and gold to the great king. The date of the campaign thus commemorated is 842 B. C., probably soon after the accession of Jehu. The Assyrian army does not appear to have actually invaded the territory of Israel; hence the tribute was sent by Jehu in the hope of strengthening his position by securing the favor of the Assyrians; but he was doomed to disappointment.

70. In this same campaign Shalmaneser met and defeated the army of Hazael near Mount Senir, a northern spur of Hermon. The camp of the Arameans, with eleven hundred and twenty-one chariots and four hundred and seventy horses, fell into the hands of the conqueror. The territory from the mountains of the Hauran to the gates of Damascus was laid waste, but the capital itself offered a successful resistance. Three years later Shalmaneser again invaded the land of Hazael, capturing four cities and receiving the tribute of Tyre and Sidon. This campaign, however, was not so extensive as the preceding, and the name of Jehu is not found among the kings who then paid tribute. Shalmaneser retired without having broken the power of Damascus. For the next thirty-five years Palestine enjoyed immunity from Assyrian invasion. The latter days of the great conqueror, Shalmaneser II., were darkened by a serious revolt headed by his oldest son. It was finally put down; but his successor, Shamshi-Ramman II., was so busily occupied in consolidating the disorganized empire that he found no time for foreign conquests.

71. This period of Assyrian inactivity Hazael im-

proved to extend the boundaries of his kingdom. Israel, being the hereditary enemy of Damascus, was naturally the first victim. Jehu, who had vainly sought deliverance by calling upon the common enemy, Assyria, bitterly atoned for his mistake. The territory of Israel east of the Jordan, and that of Moab as far as the Arnon, were overrun and made subject to Damascus (II. Kings x. 32, 33). These conquests of Hazael were characterized by extreme cruelty. The men in the conquered towns were pitilessly slain, the little children dashed in pieces, and the women subjected to the most brutal indignities (II. Kings viii. 12; Amos i. 3, 4). The Philistine town of Gath was also captured by the armies of Hazael. To reach this point they were obliged to cross the plain of Esdraelon, which they probably did as conquerors. Judah was likewise invaded, and Jerusalem was saved only by the payment of heavy tribute. During the reign of Jehu's son, Jehoahaz, the old empire of David was completely dominated by Damascus. In the graphic language of the author of Kings, the people of Israel were ground down under the heel of the conqueror until they were made "like the dust in threshing." Their fighting force was reduced to fifty horsemen, ten chariots, and ten thousand footmen. Their old foes, the Philistines, Moabites, and Edomites, took advantage of their weakness to invade their territory for the purpose of pillage and plunder, wreaking their hatred upon the defenceless, and carrying away the inhabitants to sell them into slavery (II. Kings xiii. 20, 21; Amos i. 6–15). Drought, pestilence, and famine completed their work of desolation (Amos iv. 6–11).

ISRAEL'S HUMILIATION BY DAMASCUS

72. To this period of Israel's greatest humiliation probably belongs the Elisha narrative in II. Kings vi. 24–vii. 20. It certainly has no internal relationship with the context (compare vi. 23 and viii. 1). Being a popular tradition, it unfortunately does not preserve the name of the king of Israel. The compiler of Kings, evidently considering that the Aramean king referred to was Benhadad II., who figured so prominently in Ahab's wars, assigned the narrative to its present position. More probably the invader was Benhadad III., the son of Hazael, who carried on his wars against Israel with the same energy as his older namesake (II. Kings xiii. 3). The later period also furnishes the only satisfactory background for the events recorded. The territory of Israel was completely overrun by the armies of Damascus. Its king was closely besieged within his capital, Samaria. Famine had done its work until the most unattractive food was selling for a fabulous sum. The common people, wild with hunger and despair, were even eating their own offspring. There seemed absolutely no hope of deliverance. Israel was on the verge of complete subjection.

73. Under the rule of the house of Jehu, the influence of the prophet Elisha in the court was very strong. The old antagonism between king and prophet was for a time set aside. Elisha's position and personal ability made him the chief adviser of the realm. Samaria's prolonged resistance was evidently due to his counsels, for when the king learned of the appalling conditions within the city he swore that it should cost the prophet his head. According to the narrative, Elisha met this crisis with an assurance equalled only

by that of the great Isaiah in strikingly similar circumstances (sect 152). Confidently he asserted: "Thus saith the Lord, To-morrow about this time shall a measure of fine flour be sold for a shekel, and two measures of barley for a shekel in the gate of Samaria." Before the dawn of the next day four Hebrew lepers, who had turned in desperation to the Aramean camp, came with the report that it was deserted. Subsequent investigation demonstrated that the enemy had retreated in wild confusion. The cause of their panic was the rumor that the king of Israel had hired certain allies to attack them. According to the accepted English translation, these were the Hittites and Egyptians. This may be only the popular Israelitish account of the event, while the real enemies were the Assyrians. The Hebrew word translated "Egyptians" may, however, with equal propriety be identified with the Musre, who lived to the north of the modern Syria and who are referred to several times in the Assyrian historical inscriptions. If we accept this translation, the reference is at once relieved of many of its difficulties, since the land of the Musre was near that of the Hittites, and a union between them against their hereditary enemies, the Arameans, is by no means incredible.

74. Israel would in time have been completely absorbed by the powerful kingdom of Damascus, and its independent national life extinguished, had not relief come from an unexpected quarter. The Book of Kings declares that "the Lord gave Israel a savior, so that they went out from under the hand of the Arameans" (II. Kings xiii. 5). From the monuments we learn that that savior was Assyria. Ramman-

nirari, the successor of Shamshi-Ramman, was animated by the ambitions of his predecessors. His reign of twenty-four years was filled with a series of conquests. As a result he extended the boundaries of Assyria in every direction until in the northeast it touched the Caspian Sea, and on the west the Mediterranean. About 800 B. C., Tyre, Sidon, Philistia, and Edom were reduced to subjection. The kingdom of Damascus was the most important of his western conquests. The city itself was besieged and captured, and vast plunder taken. Its king — who is called in the inscriptions "Mari," the Aramaic for "Lord" — and its people became vassals of Assyria. The "Land of Omri" (Israel) is also reckoned among the conquered states. In his campaigns, which extended to the coast of the Mediterranean, it is probable that the victorious armies of Ramman-nirari repeatedly traversed the territory of Northern Israel. Broken as it was by Aramean oppression, its ready submission to the great king was assured. It therefore bent before the storm, while Damascus, the stronger state, was shattered.

75. Joash, the son of Jehoahaz, came to the throne of Israel about 797 B. C., which was the date of the final conquest of Damascus. His accession marks a decided turn in the tide of Israel's fortunes. He conducted three successful campaigns against his old oppressor, and recovered from Damascus the Israelitish towns which had been captured in the former wars (II. Kings xiii. 17–19, 25). Amaziah of Judah, who rashly ventured to challenge him, met with a signal defeat at Bethshemesh, and was made to pay dearly for his folly. Jeroboam II., who came to the throne of

Israel about 780 B. C., inherited the energy as well as the fruits of the victories of his father, Joash. For a half-century also Palestine was relieved from the destructive attacks of Assyria. Shalmaneser III., who succeeded the great conqueror Ramman-nirari, was himself obliged to assume the defensive. Under a native prince, the Armenians, whose home was among the mountains in the north, became so formidable that they not only threw off the yoke, but also threatened the independence of Assyria. During the two succeeding reigns frequent revolts and outbreaks of pestilence exhausted still further the resources of the empire. The vassal states availed themselves of its weakness to renounce their allegiance. Among the first to do this were the principalities of Palestine.

76. During this period of freedom from foreign attack, Jeroboam II. pushed the boundaries of Israel to their farthest limits. The territory of her old rivals, the Moabites, was reconquered. Damascus was too much weakened to offer effectual resistance. The sway of Israel extended from the Arabah, on the southeastern end of the Dead Sea, to Hamath, between the Lebanons (II. Kings xiv. 25, Amos vi. 14). Judah's territory was correspondingly expanded, so that, excepting in the northeast, the ancient empire of David was again under the rule of the Hebrews. Commerce also sprang up, bringing to the Israelites wealth unheard of since the days of Solomon. The marvellous natural resources of Israel were allowed for the first time to assert themselves. This growth in property was as sudden as it was great. The nation which was trembling a generation before on the verge of annihilation had become a dominant power in the

Palestinian world. The reaction naturally induced a spirit of over-confidence in king and people. What was only Indian summer was believed to be the dawn of a golden era. In reality Assyria was only slumbering. When Damascus fell, the last barrier which protected the Israelites from this all-absorbing world-power was thrown down; the enemy was at their doors.

IV

THE PROPHETS AMOS AND HOSEA

77. AT this supreme crisis in Israel's history a new type of prophet appeared, with a new and a nobler message. Already the house of Jehu had broken loose from the principles laid down by the prophets who had called its founder to the throne. Doubtless there were many of the so-called prophets of Jehovah who stood high in royal favor, since they, like the four hundred (sect. 49), prophesied according to the will of their human rather than their divine King; but these were only imitations of the real. The distinctions between the true and false prophets were, however, not absolutely established. They were determined by the purity of the ideal revealed to each, and the steadfastness with which he adhered to it.

78. During the reign of Jeroboam II. there filled the souls of certain great prophets an ideal of national righteousness so exalted that they could only condemn the existing conditions. Reconciliation between their claims upon the nation and the policy of the reigning family was impossible. Unlike the earlier prophets, rejecting political intrigue and force, they depended entirely upon the truth of their words for their acceptance. At the same time they did not appeal to the fanaticism of the masses. Unfortunately they spoke

in an age when the authority of the prophets with the people was being rapidly destroyed by the lying messages of their false colleagues. The demands of this new class of prophets were so unfamiliar, and the principles which they annunciated so different from those generally accepted, that they were at first regarded only with suspicion. To be a true prophet during the Assyrian period required unflinching courage and unceasing patience as well as a soul open wide to divine truth. Recognizing that they could reach only a limited number by their voice, and desiring to give a permanence to their work, the prophets began regularly to commit their sermons to writing. This in itself represents a most significant transition. Only a few words, preserved in the historical narratives, were handed down to succeeding generations from the lips of the great prophets who had moulded Israel in the preceding ages. From this time on, writing became common among the Hebrews. Prophetic teaching, as a result, took more definite form. It also became cumulative, since each succeeding prophet built upon the foundations laid by his predecessors.

79. Isaiah incorporates in chapters xv. and xvi. a citation from an earlier prophecy against Moab. Tradition assigns it, on very insufficient grounds, to Jonah, the son of Amittai, who prophesied the successes of Jeroboam II. (II. Kings xiv. 25). Others also must have preceded Amos, but he is the first prophet whose prophecy and name are preserved together in the Old Testament. Although his message was to the northern kingdom, he was a native of Judah. The town of Tekoa, perched on a high hill about six miles south of Bethlehem, was his home (Amos i. 1). Im-

mediately on the east begins the wilderness of Tekoa, which extends toward the Dead Sea, twelve miles distant. The life of the town, therefore, retained the pastoral simplicity of the earlier days. Amos himself was one of the herdsmen of Tekoa. The Hebrew word indicates that he watched small animals, such as sheep and goats. The prophet also adds that he was a "dresser of sycamore trees" (vii. 14), probably at the proper season piercing their fruit that it might ripen so as to be utilized as food by the poor, who could secure nothing more palatable. Hence his occupation was the humblest. His surroundings were all pastoral and agricultural. His prophecy also abounds in figures drawn from the simple life of the country. At the same time he betrays a familiarity with lands outside Judah, which must have been the result of personal observation. The peculiar location of Samaria and the conditions within Israel's capital were well known to him (iii. 9, 10). His references to the surrounding nations reveal an intimate acquaintance with them (i., ii.). The graphic allusion to the rising and falling of Egypt's river suggests that this shepherd-prophet had sometime made a journey to that wonderland.

80. By environment and observation, therefore, this earnest man of Judah was prepared for his great mission. He does not tell us when or how it was that "Jehovah took him from following the flock and said unto him, 'Go prophesy unto my people Israel'" (vii. 15). Perhaps it gradually dawned upon his slowly awakening spiritual consciousness. The fact remains that when — about the middle of the eighth century B. C. — one festal day he began to preach to

the crowds of Israelites who gathered at their great national sanctuary, Bethel, he was absolutely certain of his God-given commission. To their angry, suspicious looks, inquiring what right he, a rude Judean shepherd, had to condemn them, he replied: "You certainly will agree that a lion does not roar in the forest when it hath no prey, and that a bird does not fall into a snare where none has been set; in other words, that nothing unusual occurs without a corresponding cause; consequently, my presence here is conclusive evidence that I was sent. On the other hand, — I appeal to you who recall the awful wars with Damascus — Is the trumpet, announcing that the enemy is near, ever blown without the people being afraid? Every sufficient cause produces a corresponding effect. You all believe that when evil comes to a city, it is the Lord who sends it. Furthermore, you know that God does nothing which he does not reveal unto his servants the prophets. When the Lord God speaks to a prophet, as he has to me, you must know that prophet can do nothing but prophesy" (iii. 3–8).

81. Coming thus, a foreigner without introduction, to sing in the ears of a self-satisfied, prosperous people the death-dirge, "The virgin Israel is fallen no more to rise," Amos showed marvellous skill in his opening address. In a series of short prophecies, in which the recurring formulas add to the effectiveness, he denounces the sins of Israel's enemies, and proclaims that at last they have sinned beyond forgiveness, and that, therefore, destruction impends. This was joyful news to his hearers. They listen eagerly; but in giving their ready assent they unwittingly subscribed to certain principles which the prophet forthwith applied

to their own case with awful effectiveness. His logic was so unassailable, and their iniquities which he denounced so patent, that the rulers and priests of the proud royal sanctuary were obliged to listen without interruption, until at last he declared, "The sanctuaries of Israel shall be laid waste; and I will rise against the house of Jeroboam with the sword" (vii. 9). This gave an opportunity for a charge of blasphemy and treason, which Amaziah, the priest of Bethel, hastened to improve. "Amos hath conspired against thee in the midst of the house of Israel; the land is not able to bear all his words. For thus Amos saith, Jeroboam shall die by the sword, and Israel shall surely be led away captive out of the land" (vii. 10, 11), was the message, half truth, half falsehood, which he sent to Jeroboam. Either on his own authority or that of the king, Amaziah then turned upon Amos with the sarcastic words: "O thou seer, go, flee thee away into the land of Judah, and there eat bread, and prophesy there; but prophesy not again any more at Bethel; for it is the king's sanctuary, and it is a royal house" (vii. 12, 13). Disclaiming the implication that he was one of those mercenary prophets who "declare war against those who put not bribes in their mouth" (Micah iii. 5), he protested that he was only a humble shepherd whom Jehovah called from his occupation and sent upon the present mission (vii. 14, 15). He was compelled to depart; but even as he turned to leave he took occasion to reiterate most impressively the burden of his message: "Thou and thy family, O Amaziah, shall experience all the bitter woes of conquest, and Israel shall surely be led away captive out of his land."

NATIONALITY AND CHARACTER OF HOSEA 83

82. Amos returned to his flock. A few of the more thoughtful in Israel pondered over his solemn words of warning; but the majority only remembered that at a certain feast at Bethel one of those fanatical prophets, betrayed by his accent and manners to be a Judean shepherd, had startled them all for a time by his awful denunciations, until at last the priest, Amaziah, had silenced the mad fellow. The truth, however, which had once found expression could not be long silenced. During the latter part of the reign of Jeroboam, Hosea, the son of Beeri, also began to preach to his countrymen. His reference to "our king" (vii. 5), who must have been one of the rulers of Israel, his familiarity with the geography and history, and, above all, the loyal love for the northern kingdom which he shows in every utterance, indicate beyond question that, unlike Amos, he was a citizen of the greater Hebrew state. His illustrations and references suggest that his home was in a large town or city. From his familiarity with the early traditions of his people (i. 4; viii. 14; x. 6, 9, 10; xi. 1; xii. 12; xiii. 4), it may be inferred that he was a careful student of its history. The style and thought of his prophecies reveal a loving, sympathetic nature, sensitive and tender as that of a woman. His feelings are often so deep that they only find utterance in broken and disconnected sentences. His logic is that of the emotions and intuitions rather than of reason.

83. From the allusions contained in the first three chapters of his prophecy, it is possible to reconstruct the outlines of his sad private history. Like many other prophets, in response to the promptings of true affection, he took to himself as wife a woman by the

name of Gomer, the daughter of Diblaim. He believed that she would faithfully return the strong love which he felt toward her; but later experience proved that she, like so many of the Israelitish women of that age, was indeed one of "the daughters of whoredom." Law and custom permitted him to put her away, but his love and the hope that he could yet reclaim her led him to forgive the heinous crime. Even after she fled from his home with her paramour, and was finally put up for sale as a common slave, he bought and restored her to his home, so darkened by her infamy. Then by discipline, which is sometimes the supreme proof of love toward the erring, he sought to lead her back to the path of rectitude. Whether he succeeded or not, he does not add; but these simple, sad facts, presented with a purpose, reveal the method whereby Divine Love spoke to Hosea. His own tragic experience enabled him to appreciate Jehovah's feeling toward apostate Israel, which he likewise had loved, called, forgiven, and finally, as a last resort, was forced to punish, that the people might be led in penitence to claim his forgiveness. Hosea knew, as did no other man in Israel, the pain which the sin of one who is loved can bring to the heart of the one loving. This explains why his denunciations of sinful Israel are unequalled for their vehemence. On the other hand, his messages of divine love and mercy are the strongest and the tenderest uttered by Hebrew prophet. His public as well as his private life was a tragedy of tragedies, for it was his sad fate to proclaim saving truth to his beloved nation and then see it rapidly go down to its ruin, simply because it refused to listen. In this painful school of affliction, however, Hosea learned lessons which make his obscure, broken prophecy the gospel of the Old Testament.

84. These two prophets were despised and rejected by their contemporaries. Hosea bitterly complains that the prophet who denounces Israel's sins is regarded as a fool, and the man that hath a spirit as mad (ix. 7). The prophet is subjected on every side to treacherous and murderous attacks; even in the house of his God he does not escape from the malignity of his relentless foes (ix. 8). His life was one long martyrdom. The rulers of Israel paid no more heed to the words of Amos and Hosea, than to the barking of the dogs without their capital city; and yet time has proved that the prophets were right and the rulers wrong. Unquestionably they are the most important figures in the last act of Israel's drama; for the activity of the Hebrew prophets ultimately moulded their nation's history, and thereby distinguished it from that of the hundred other petty states which rose and fell, and have long since been forgotten.

V

SOCIETY AND MORALS IN ISRAEL

85. ISRAEL'S sudden fall from the height of prosperity which it enjoyed under Jeroboam II. was not entirely due to the cruelty of the foreign conqueror. To use a prophetic figure, the nation was like an attractive basket of rich tropical fruit, dead ripe; it was fair to look upon, but within were the germs of decay, which were destined in a short time, under unfavorable conditions, to transform it into a mass of loathsome putrefaction (Amos viii. 1–3). The prophets, detecting, by the aid of their enlightened vision, these insidious evils, pointed them out and at the same time suggested the remedy. Amos, viewing conditions in Israel as a foreigner, directed his attention almost exclusively to social questions; while Hosea, who was able to go to the roots of the nation's life, was constantly dealing with its morals and religion.

86. Certain social disorders, to which an Oriental community, organized like the Hebrew states, was especially susceptible, were constantly breaking out in Israel. The principles underlying the Hebrew commonwealth were essentially democratic. During its early history questions of national interest were settled in a popular assembly, or in a representative

council of the tribal elders. The king was chosen by the people to be their servant. Every free Israelite had inalienable rights which the king must respect. Judicial as well as political power was delegated. A Hebrew judge, like the sheik of a modern Bedouin tribe, was little more than a referee. Custom supplied the place of a constitution and legal code. Right and justice were therefore guarded, not by law and political organization, but by the co-operation of all the citizens of the community. Anything which destroyed the simple and normal relations of its individual members shook the very foundations of the state. Earlier prophets recognized this fact. When the old simplicity was threatened under Solomon and Ahab, they strove to maintain it at any cost, and for the time succeeded. Tendencies, however, were at work which the prophets with their waning political influence could no longer stay.

87. History proves that the chief burden of a protracted, intense struggle, such as was the war between Israel and Damascus, rests upon the middle and poorer classes. Year after year, they were obliged to go forth for the defence of their families, while their little estates were neglected. They returned to find their hereditary lands consumed and themselves and families reduced to slavery. When the tide of war turned and the spoil of conquest poured into Israel, it did not materially relieve the poor. Instead it merely enriched the military nobility which had arisen during the long years of war. Commerce, which sprang up in a time of peace, only added to the wealth of the already rich, increasing the distance between classes. Thus it was that the old simplicity, so essential to such

a state as Israel, suddenly disappeared, and with it the middle class, who are the main dependence of every nation, leaving only the rich nobility and their poor dependants.

88. Unwonted national prosperity aroused among the rich and powerful in Israel a passion for show and luxury which was the more striking because of the contrast with the simplicity of the earlier days and the want and penury which were still the lot of the masses. Great estates took the place of small holdings; palaces of hewn stone, furnished with beds of ivory and silken couches, rose on the land once held by the families of those who now were serfs (Amos iii. 11, 12; v. 11; vi. 4). Their idle masters sought far and wide for the choicest morsels with which to gratify their appetites, as they stretched themselves upon their ivory couches, singing idle songs to the sound of the viol, anointing themselves with expensive ointment and engaging in shameful carousals (Amos vi. 1-7). It was a selfish luxury which led those who thus indulged themselves to disregard entirely the sacred duty which they owed to their poorer brethren (Amos vi. 6). Instead it led them to deeds of inhuman cruelty, in comparison with which the barbarity of the heathen nations about them, which they so readily condemned, could easily be condoned (Amos i.-iii.). A poor debtor, even though he was a righteous man and his indebtedness a mere trifle, received not the least mercy at their hands; indeed, they exulted in the misery which they brought upon him (Amos ii. 6, 7; viii. 4). Their chief delight seemed to be to wrong the needy and helpless (Amos ii. 7). Their palaces were filled with the fruits of

their violence and robbery (Amos iii. 10). Even the wives of the nobles, those from whom mercy might be expected, if from any source, only "oppressed the poor and crushed the needy" by urging their husbands on to greater exactions, in order to gratify their unholy appetites. The public tribunals, instead of being sources of justice, were made the instruments whereby the rulers extracted bribes and perverted the cause of the poor and helpless (Amos v. 12). Under such conditions there could be no harmony between classes, nor unity in the state. There is a grim significance in the message of Amaziah to the king respecting Amos's plain unveiling of Israel's social evils: "Amos hath conspired against thee in the midst of the house of Israel: The land is not able to bear all his words." Even the ruling class realized that only a leader was necessary to set the much wronged masses into a mad revolt. When such conditions existed within the nation, there was no hope of escape from the clutches of the foreign foe.

89. At a later and more degenerate period, when the strong hand of Jeroboam II. no longer guided the state, Hosea brought in a still more sweeping indictment against Israel: "There is no truth, nor mercy, nor knowledge of God in the land. There is naught but swearing, and breaking faith, and killing, and stealing, and committing adultery; they break out, and deeds of bloodshed touch deeds of bloodshed" (iv. 1, 2). Israel's crimes were those common among all peoples, but especially so in the Orient. Repeatedly Hosea complains that the people swear falsely in making covenants, and that the deceit which characterized their forefather Jacob has not ceased to be

the besetting sin of his descendants (x. 4; xi. 12). It found expression in the false measures and balances which Amos saw in the hands of the merchants of Israel (viii. 5). Theft and highway robbery were common (Hosea vii. 1). Rulers, prophets, and priests, who were the appointed guardians of the people, conspired together to spoil them (Hosea v. 1; iv. 6; vi. 9). Anarchy ruled unchallenged (Amos iii. 9; Hosea vii. 5-7). In this atmosphere, so deeply tainted by the influence of Baalism, there flourished a gross immorality which extended to all classes. The daughters of Israel gave themselves up to the licentious practices attendant upon that degenerate cult (Hosea iv. 11-15). Deeds of lewdness, such as would have aroused public indignation even in the barbarous days of the judges, were of common occurrence (Hosea ix. 9; x. 9: Judges xix.). The most sacred laws of society were wantonly disregarded (Amos ii. 7).

90. The virgin Israel indeed had fallen so low that there was little hope that she would ever rise again (Amos v. 2). In the last chapter of the prophecy of Amos the firm conviction is expressed that after captivity had sifted out the evil elements in the state, the few faithful would be restored to enjoy a peace and prosperity far surpassing that of the earlier days (ix. 8-15). Hosea also pictured, in rich imagery, the glorious era which would be inaugurated when once Israel's discipline had accomplished its end and the people had come back to Jehovah in penitence to be reconciled to him "in righteousness and in judgment and in loving-kindness and in mercies" (ii. 9-23). Both prophets, however, as they saw the social and moral degeneracy of the nation, and the blind self-

confidence of its leaders, which gave no promise of reform, declared that its destruction at the hands of a foreign conqueror was absolutely certain (Amos iv. 12; vi. 14; vii. 9; Hosea iii. 3, 4; xiii. 16). The Judean prophets, Isaiah and Micah, echoed the same (Isaiah xxviii. 1-13; Micah i. 2-7). Subsequent developments confirmed most signally their inspired diagnosis of Israel's sickness, and established the eternal principles upon which they based their predictions.

VI

POPULAR AND PROPHETIC RELIGION

91. THE blackness of the picture wherein Amos and Hosea portray the social and moral conditions of their age is undoubtedly in part due to the striking contrast between their standards and those of their contemporaries. The masses still clung to the old conception of Jehovah. They believed that he was simply Israel's god and stood in the same relation to them as Chemosh did to the Moabites (I. sects. 72, 167). The series of national misfortunes which had befallen them were regarded as tokens of his displeasure (Amos iv. 6-11). The turn in the tide of war which brought to them the unparalleled prosperity of the reign of Jeroboam II. was regarded as conclusive evidence that Jehovah was pleased with his people. Starting with the mistaken dogma, then already old, that success was always a proof of divine favor, and calamity of displeasure, they, as was the hero of the Book of Job when oppressed by the same error, must often have been forced to the conclusion that Jehovah, like the gods of the Greeks, was at times ruled by caprice. Ordinarily, however, they believed, as did Mesha, king of Moab (compare Moabite Inscription), that zealous service by sword and sacrifice would surely secure his

favor. On the other hand, according to the naïve thought of the age, Israel was the one people of Jehovah, therefore his glory was dependent upon their national prosperity. Adversity might afflict them for a time, but erelong he would surely arouse himself to deliver them and vindicate his honor among their foes, who were also his enemies (Amos v. 18). Assyrian storm clouds lowered in the distant horizon, but the mass of the Israelites felt absolutely sure that Jehovah would deliver; for, according to their conception of him, it was incredible that he would allow his people, who alone of all the nations bore his name, to be destroyed. Besides, were they not honoring him with a devotion and wealth of sacrifice unequalled before in their history? The cry, "My God, we, Israel, know thee" (Hosea viii. 2), voiced the popular feeling. They deemed the one who predicted the downfall of Israel guilty of impious blasphemy.

92. Such a religion put little stress upon social or private morality. While Jehovah was served by ceremony and offering, that sufficed. The ordinary priests and prophets encouraged the people in this fatal delusion. Amaziah, the chief priest of the royal sanctuary at Bethel, regarded the teaching of Amos as the wildest fanaticism (Amos vii. 12, 13). Hosea declared to the priesthood, "Thou shalt stumble in the day, and the prophet also shall stumble with thee in the night. ... My people are destroyed for lack of knowledge. I have rejected thee, that thou shalt be no priest to me; seeing thou hast forgotten the law of thy God, I also will forget thy children. As they were multiplied, so they sinned against me; I will change their glory into shame. They feed on the sin

of my people, and set their hearts on iniquity. And it shall be, like people, like priest" (iv. 5-9). They were but blind leaders of the blind. The ceremonial service itself was attended by mad revels (Amos v. 23; Hosea iv. 11-14; ix. 1-5). The priests of the different sanctuaries vied with one another in making their services the most attractive, in order to swell the offerings. Their greed made them little better than highway robbers (Hosea vi. 9). When the national religion was so corrupt, we cease to wonder that society was so rotten.

93. The miracle, explicable only as we recognize the influence of the Divine, is that certain prophets were led to reject completely the prevailing ideas, and to present a system of faith and morals which has become the foundation of the three greatest world religions. Amos outlines, in his artistic introduction (i., ii.), the new and revolutionizing principles which characterize his prophecy. Jehovah rules, not only over Israel, but over each and every nation. The gods of the other peoples shrivel into insignificance in the full light of this truth. Before Jehovah's tribunal the nations are condemned, because they have transgressed the common laws of humanity. Each is judged according to its enlightenment. Hence greater privilege entails greater responsibility. Jehovah is a righteous God, and therefore demands righteousness from his people, and can show no favoritism. Having gained a half-assent to these profound propositions, Amos proceeded to throw down in quick succession the cherished fallacies which hitherto had dominated the minds of the Israelites. "Yes, you alone of all the peoples of the world have I known in a peculiarly intimate

relation," declares Jehovah, "but because your opportunities have been greater, I will visit upon you all your iniquities (iii. 2). Jehovah despises all your feasts and sacrifices and ceremonial worship, because they are mere mockery, when accompanied, as they are, with deeds of injustice and inhumanity (iv. 4, 5; v. 21–25). He is no human judge who can be bribed with gifts. Righteousness is the only acceptable offering. Do you not know that he has also been active in the life of other nations? He it was that brought your hereditary enemies, the Philistines, from Caphtor, and the Arameans from Kir, just as he led you out of Egypt (ix. 7.) In fact, it is he who is bringing this great nation, Assyria, to execute upon you the death sentence" (vi. 14).

94. It is not strange that the Israelites were unable to comprehend a message which swept away their immemorial claims to Jehovah's especial favor, and placed them in such unfavorable contrast with their hated enemies. Amos was indeed an iconoclast; but whence his new truth? The situation suggests the means whereby the Eternal revealed himself to his prophets. The first element in the revelation was that they saw existing conditions in their true significance. They recognized that the advance of Assyria meant destruction for Israel. In the face of this fact, the old conceptions of Jehovah as merely the god of a land and people were totally insufficient, for they offered only one explanation: the God of Israel was no God, or else weaker than the gods of the conquering race. This was the conclusion which the exiled Israelites accepted, and thereby forfeited their national individuality and religion (sect. 104). Confronted by the

same burning question, Amos was divinely led to open his eyes and see instead of the God of Israel the God of the universe, who directed the march of the Assyrian armies as well as fought for Israel. With this came a full grasp of the truth, heretofore but imperfectly enunciated, that Jehovah was a God of perfect righteousness. A study of conditions within Israel soon revealed the reason of the approaching captivity. Henceforth devotion to the ideal of righteousness, even though it cost the life of their state, characterized the true prophets. With untiring zeal they strove to realize it in their nation, and at the same time endeavored to prepare their race for the great catastrophe which they saw approaching. It was due to their unceasing efforts that the spark of national life and faith was kept alive during the trying centuries which followed.

95. Hosea reiterated the teachings of his predecessor, and added many new and precious truths. Amos had looked with no favor upon the religious cult of Israel; Hosea, appreciating its debasing influence, unhesitatingly denounced the worship of the golden calves as wholly corrupt (viii. 5; x. 5; xiii. 2, 3). With infinite tenderness, he called upon the Israelites to forsake "the work of their own hands" and turn to a God in whom "the fatherless findeth mercy," who would "heal their backslidings and love them freely" (xiv. 3, 4). As we have seen (sect. 83), Hosea's tragic private experience was that which prepared him to appreciate the character and purpose of Jehovah even more truly than Amos. The God whom he proclaimed was righteous because he was loving. He declared that the approaching captivity was to be not merely a

fulfilment of the stern laws of justice, but rather a form of discipline intended to call the nation back to repentance (ii. 10-23; iii. 4, 5). The punishment brought far less pain to Israel than to the loving heart of Jehovah. Gladly would he remit the penalty if love did not command that it be executed (xi. 8-9). The stern, just God of Amos assumes an entirely different aspect, and through the eyes of Hosea we behold a Divine Father, who with infinite love and tenderness called "his son [Israel] from Egypt, taught him to walk, and took him in his arms." Although the child was wayward, he drew him "with the bands of love" (xi. 1-4). Again the figure changes and Jehovah is the husband who sought out Israel and was united to the nation by the sacred covenant bonds. With unceasing love, he anticipated Israel's every want, although it was requited only with the basest infidelity and ingratitude. Whenever the discipline of captivity should bring the foolish, erring people back to Jehovah, he stood ready to forgive and to restore (ii. 1-23). Thus, while the masses blindly worshipped a tribal god, whose favor and help they sought to win by the abundance of their gifts, Amos perceived that Jehovah was the righteous ruler of the universe; and Hosea, with still deeper insight, proclaimed the supreme truth of religion, that God is love.

VII

THE DECLINE AND FALL OF ISRAEL

96. WHILE the prophets were learning from the great crisis through which their nation was passing new and rich lessons, Israel was rapidly hastening to its ruin. Jeroboam died about 740 B. C., and in less than two decades the proud kingdom over which he ruled ceased to exist. Four of the six kings who succeeded him were struck down by assassins, and one died in captivity. His son, Zechariah, perished by a conspiracy, after a reign of only six months. Shallum, the chief conspirator, reigned in the capital a month, and then was slain by Menahem, the son of Gadi, who appears to have been the military governor of the old Israelitish capital of Tirzah. His rule, like that of Omri, was at first opposed, but he succeeded in subjugating the disaffected districts, and then visited upon them a most brutal revenge (II. Kings xv. 16). The weakness of his position is indicated by the statement of the Book of Kings to the effect that he gave a thousand talents of silver, which he exacted from the wealthy in his realm, to Pul to confirm the kingdom in his hand (II. Kings xv. 19, 20). Although Pul is not mentioned in the Assyrian annals, it is established from other sources that he was Tiglath-Pileser III.,

who reigned on the throne of Assyria from 745 to 727 B. C., — Pul being his private name and Tiglath-Pileser the official title which he assumed and which of course is always employed on the monuments.

97. This was the great conqueror who revived the waning fortunes of the Assyrian empire. His connection with the old reigning family, if any, was distant, since in the annals no reference is made to his ancestry. He succeeded, by infusing into his nation new blood and energy, in organizing again its resources and kindling its old ambitions for conquest. The first six years of his reign were occupied with campaigns in the east; but before 738 B. C. he had broken the strength of the kingdom of Hamath, north of Israel, and of its ally, Azariah (Uzziah) of Judah (sect. 126), and in that year reached the borders of Israel. The inscriptions, therefore, give the date at which Israel paid tribute, as well as confirm the biblical record, since they state that among the many western princes who then acknowledged his suzerainty were Rezon of Damascus, Menahem of Samaria, and Hiram of Tyre. The Assyrian empire again touched the Mediterranean. The two great world powers, with their capitals on the Tigris and the Nile, stood face to face. Palestine, being the key to both the east and the west, was the bone of contention.

98. From this time on, Israel and Judah were to be the scene of constant intrigue and war. Ephraim, "like a silly dove," flew blindly into the Assyrian net (Hosea vii. 11). Menahem's weak, selfish policy gave the great eastern power a hold upon Israel which was never relaxed. Inordinate greed, as well as insatiable cruelty, characterized the conquering nation. Each year

the resources of Israel were drained to pay the heavy tribute which was exacted. The nation writhed under the awful injustice. Egypt, jealous of the influence of her rival, was constantly holding out promises of assistance in case Israel would revolt. Although the prophets pointed out the folly of such an alliance (Hosea vii. 11; xii. 1), and the weakness of Egypt was evident, a large and growing party advocated the plan of throwing off the yoke of Assyria, and of trusting to their own strength and the support of Egypt to resist the common foe. Menahem and his son, however, led the opposite faction, which might be called the Assyrian party, since it urged that safety was to be found only in submission. For about five years they maintained their policy. The second part of the prophecies of Hosea reflects something of the confusion and weakness which characterized the period. The king and princes regarded the people as their prey (v. 1), law and order were relaxed, and with this a wild abandon took possession of all classes (vii. 8–16). Under such conditions the strength of the anti-Assyrian party increased rapidly. It found a leader in Pekah, the son of Remaliah, the captain of Pekahiah who succeeded his father, Menahem. Supported by fifty of his fearless Gileadite followers, he raised the standard of revolt in Samaria and slew the inefficient king. The year 735 B. C. must have been the date of this revolution.

99. That which encouraged the Israelites to strike for independence at this time was undoubtedly the absence of Tiglath-Pileser III. and his armies, since we learn from his annals that he was engaged, between 737 and 735 B. C., in campaigns in the east. Rezon of

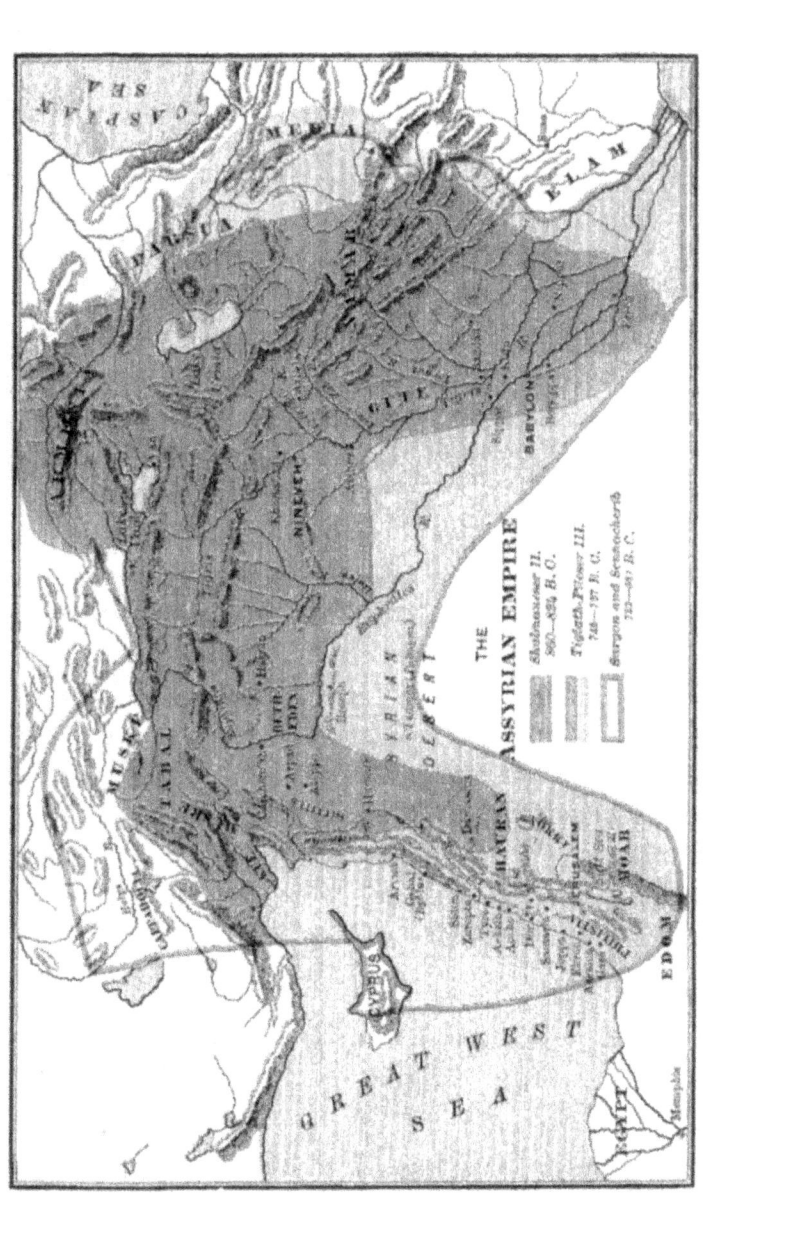

Damascus, and the Philistine cities, Askelon and Gaza, joined with Pekah in a coalition against Assyria. The other peoples of Syria, however, held aloof. The allies recognized that the only hope of successful resistance lay in a union of all. Accordingly they marched against Judah, to force it to join with them. Its territory was devastated, and its king shut up in his capital; but before he could be brought to submission Tiglath-Pileser with his armies was upon the rebels. His advance was so rapid that they were taken unprepared. He followed the usual route along the coast of the Mediterranean. From the west he sent his armies eastward over the plain of Esdraelon, and from thence to the conquest of the Israelitish towns in the north. Ijon, Abel-beth-maacah, Janoah, Kedesh, and Hazor are the cities mentioned in the biblical record (II. Kings xv. 29). All this territory north of the plain of Esdraelon was subjugated and placed under the charge of Assyrian governors. Continuing his march southward, he captured Askelon and Gaza, thereby securing the frontiers of Palestine and cutting off all possibility of assistance from Egypt. Returning, he completed the subjugation of Israel. The territory of Ephraim was devastated, and many of its inhabitants carried away captive. The rebel Pekah, who had made such a valiant though ineffectual strike for freedom, was put to death. According to II. Kings xv. 30, the Israelite Hoshea, whom Tiglath-Pileser appointed governor over the remnant of Israel, probably as a reward for his treason, was the instrument whereby Pekah met his end.

100. This memorable campaign of 734 B. C. gave Israel its death-blow. Its territory was henceforth

limited to a few square miles, bounded on the north by the plain of Esdraelon and on the east by the Jordan. Although stripped of their wealth, those who were allowed to remain behind were compelled to pay an exorbitant annual tribute to Assyria. During the two succeeding years Damascus suffered a similar fate. Its army was defeated, and its king shut up in his capital "like a caged bird." Its territory, even to the walls of the city, was laid waste with a thoroughness of which the Assyrians alone were capable. In 732 B. C. Damascus itself fell (compare II. Kings xvi. 9). In accordance with the policy of Tiglath-Pileser III. and his successors, its people were deported to the northern part of the Assyrian empire. In this effective way its power was extinguished so that it never again gave serious annoyance to its conquerors. Even before Tiglath-Pileser appeared, Ahaz of Judah had hastened to swear allegiance; the kings of Edom, Moab, and Ammon later followed his example. Tiglath-Pileser also made a successful incursion into Arabia, reducing to subjection a strong tribe under a queen by the name of Samsi, and received the homage and tribute of many Arabian chiefs. By his skill and energy he had not only completely reorganized the decaying empire, but also had extended its boundaries far beyond all former limits.

101. As long as the great conqueror lived, Hoshea, the governor, whom he had placed over the remnant who still bore the name of Israel, remained faithful; but the death of Tiglath-Pileser III. in 727 B. C. was the signal for a general revolt. Shalmaneser IV., his successor, anticipated this by despatching an army into the west-land. Under the pressure of these circum-

stances, Hoshea did homage and brought tribute to his new master; but when the army was withdrawn he yielded to the demands of the anti-Assyrian party. He was only a vassal king of the crippled remnant of a little nation, while Assyria was at its height. Already the toils of the world-conqueror had been tightened by the fruitless efforts which the Israelites had made to gain their freedom. If they failed, all was lost, for the next stage of subjection was deportation and national annihilation. Judah was neither willing nor able to render any aid. It was Egypt's empty promises which encouraged the feverish leaders of the northern kingdom to court certain destruction. About this time also the kings of Ethiopia, whose power had long overshadowed that of the weak rulers of northern Egypt, took possession of the throne of the Pharaohs. With the new dynasty the old longings for conquest were revived. The first step toward their realization was an attempt to undermine the influence of their dangerous rival in Palestine. This was in part successful, for the name of Egypt still inspired confidence, and the renown of the new Pharaoh, Shabaka, aroused unwarranted hopes.

102. In 725 or 724 B. C. the fatal alliance was formed between Hoshea and his would-be patron (II. Kings xvii. 4). Before any relief came from Egypt, Shalmaneser IV. invaded Israel and captured its king, who apparently had advanced against him. The details respecting the events of the last few years of the northern kingdom are exceedingly meagre. Although deprived of their king, its leaders made a last stand in Samaria. Its impregnable position made it impossible for the Assyrians to capture it by storm,

and therefore they were obliged to wait three years until starvation had done its ghastly work. The rich territory about was all in the hands of the enemy, so that there was no hope of relief from their countrymen. The expectation that Egypt would yet deliver them, and the knowledge that they could anticipate no mercy from their conqueror, nerved them for a heroic though hopeless resistance. The crowded city must have been the scene of the most horrible want and misery. Egypt's weakness and disorganized condition rendered it utterly incapable of coping with the thoroughly equipped, experienced armies of Assyria; indeed, there is no evidence that it made any attempt to help its ally. Shalmaneser began and practically completed the conquest of Samaria, but, dying before the city finally surrendered, its capture was one of the first events which rendered glorious the reign of the great conqueror, Sargon, who succeeded him in December of 722 B. C. The policy of assimilation inaugurated by Tiglath-Pileser III. was carried out even more rigidly by the new monarch. The city was given up to plunder; twenty-seven thousand two hundred and ninety of its inhabitants were, according to the inscriptions of Sargon, carried away into captivity, and over those who were left behind was placed an Assyrian governor to attend to the collection of the annual tribute. Section after section of the kingdom of Jeroboam II. had been broken off and annexed to Assyria, until at the end of eighteen years the capital itself was brought under the same iron sway and Israel as a nation ceased to exist.

VIII

THE RÔLE OF ISRAEL IN THE WORLD'S HISTORY

103. WITH the fall of Samaria, Israel not only lost its identity as a nation, but the character of its people also was completely changed under the influence of the foreign populations which surged into the land. Assyria's policy of eradicating by force all national spirit and of assimilating and amalgamating the different races in its vast empire, that the possibility of revolt might be removed, ultimately proved eminently successful in the case of Israel. In 720 B. C., two years after the fall of Samaria, there was a general uprising in Syria, which included Hamath, Arpad, and Damascus. The provinces into which the land of Israel had been divided were drawn into the insurrection. The severity of the penalty which was inflicted upon the Israelites was probably in part due to this additional offence. Strategic reasons also prompted Sargon to root out completely all possible seeds of rebellion, since the strong fortress of Samaria commanded central Palestine; and already Assyrian plans of conquest extended beyond Syria to Egypt.

104. The captives who were deported naturally included the rich, the ruling and military classes, and the religious leaders. One body of exiles was settled

on the chief northern tributary of the Euphrates, the river Habor, within the Mesopotamian province of Gozan. Here they were surrounded by an Aramaic-speaking population, with which they readily assimilated, and consequently quickly lost their identity. Another group was transported, several years later, to the land of the Medes, on the extreme eastern borders of the empire. The location, Halah, the third place mentioned in II. Kings xvii. 6, has not yet been definitely established; it may have been situated in Mesopotamia, or possibly east of the Tigris. The great majority of the Israelites who survived the devastating Assyrian wars were allowed to remain in their homes. The pastoral and agricultural classes in the community suffered least. Since the territory north of the plain of Esdraelon submitted first and with little resistance, it escaped the repeated deportations which so seriously modified the character of the population of the district lying to the south. This fact explains why, after the exile, the Galileans affiliated with the Jews so much more readily than did the Samaritans.

105. According to II. Kings xvii. 24, " The king of Assyria brought men from Babylon, and from Cuthah, and from Avva, and from Hamath, and from Sepharvaim, and placed them in the cities of Samaria instead of the children of Israel; and they possessed Samaria, and dwelt in the cities thereof." The annals of Sargon corroborate and supplement this reference. Among the events of his first year, it is stated that colonists from the rebellious state of Babylon were transported to the land of the Hittites, which was a general designation of Syria. Cuthah and Sepharvaim have been

identified as Babylonian towns. During the second year of Sargon's reign, Hamath, having rebelled, was subjected to the severest punishment known to the conqueror. Colonists from the east were introduced to take the place of the natives, who, according to the biblical record, were transferred to Samaria. Two other inscriptions state that Arabians from four desert tribes conquered by Sargon were also settled in Samaria. About half a century later Esarhaddon transported thither still other colonists from Babylonia and the cities of Elam (Ezra iv. 2, 9, 10). A more heterogeneous mixture of peoples could not be imagined; Babylonians, Elamites, Arabians, and Hamatheans mingled their blood with that of the ancient Israelites to form the Samaritan race which was thus gradually evolved. Their national spirit was so completely crushed that they submitted readily to the various foreign conquerors who have ever since ruled the land of Palestine. The result has been that they alone, of all the ancient peoples who once inhabited this much contested territory, have survived, and today are represented by a small tribe of about one hundred members, who live together at Nablus, the ancient Shechem, and on their sacred Mount Gerizim worship Jehovah in accordance with the customs of their fathers.

106. It is obvious that the wild theories concerning the fate of the "lost ten tribes of Israel" are entirely without foundation, since they were never lost. Their descendants survived and at times emerged into prominence; but with the destruction of Samaria in 722 B. C., the Israelites sank to the level of the peoples about them. The catastrophe, which the true prophets

had labored so earnestly to avert, came at last. The foreign colonists worshipped their respective gods for a time; but, in accord with the current ideas of the age, public disasters were soon interpreted as an indication that the god of the land was angry. Therefore priests of Jehovah were introduced; Bethel again became a religious centre; the worship of the God of Israel continued to be the acknowledged cult of the land; but other gods were freely tolerated, and Jehovah was regarded as little more than a local divinity and placed on an equality with the other deities. The old heathen forms were also retained. The conception of Jehovah ceasing to develop, the religion itself became dead; and when its faith was dead, Israel's life was no longer an important factor in the history of humanity. Its glory and its influence came alone from its past.

107. The sudden and disastrous fate of Israel explains why a comparatively small part of the literature of the Old Testament comes from the larger Hebrew kingdom. That kingdom fell just as the Hebrews were entering upon their most prolific literary period. The Judeans, who became the custodians of its writings, were never very kindly disposed toward the people of the north, and the feeling of antagonism steadily increased during the succeeding centuries. In view of these facts, it is surprising that so much has been preserved. Probably a few of the proverbs and psalms in our present collections are from Israelitish authors. The Song of Songs breathes the spirit and reflects the point of view of the north rather than of the south. One of the most important strands of prophetic narrative (E) which run through the Hexateuch, bears

unmistakable marks of its Israelitish origin. Almost all the ancient material preserved in the Book of Judges, part of that in Samuel, and the greater portion of Kings were derived originally from northern sources. Although the prophet Amos was a Judean, his message was directed wholly against the north, and may properly be reckoned among its literature. The prophecy of Hosea is at the same time the noblest and most characteristic product of Israel. Although its style is rough and broken, its figures and references suggest something of the beauty and delicacy of thought which under brighter skies find expression in the Song of Songs, and which might have come to perfection, had not the fruits of the nation's sins and adverse circumstances forever silenced its poets and prophets.

108. Until Samaria began to totter, the spiritual side of the religion of Jehovah found its true development in Israel. Religiously as well as politically, the southern kingdom followed in the wake of the greater and more active state. Israel alone had an Elijah and an Elisha. The great religious and social crisis arose first in the north. Its enlightened prophets gave the watchwords to all who followed. The definite proclamation by Amos, that Jehovah was the God of the universe and at the same time altogether righteous, ultimately revolutionized religious thought. He also first clearly enunciated the great fact of the universal brotherhood of man, and emphasized the obligations which grow out of it. When he declared that ceremonial service was hateful to God if unaccompanied by deeds of justice and mercy, he presented a truth which humanity has not yet fully grasped. Hosea first saw

clearly that love, not arbitrary will, rules the universe, and announced that Jehovah is just because his love is supreme. He recognized the Supreme Father of mankind, and in his messages of warning to the nation and in his promises of God's forgiveness laid the foundations of the New Testament revelation. Israel's greatest prophets stand apart and above their nation; the truths which they proclaimed were never accepted and consequently never realized in its history; but in Judah, and ultimately in the life of humanity, they found their true field of development. Israel therefore, through the messages of its prophets, enjoys immortality, although its body politic met such an untimely death.

PART III

THE ASSYRIAN PERIOD OF JUDAH'S HISTORY

I

THE HISTORICAL SOURCES, AND CHRONOLOGY

109. SIDE by side with the material contained in II. Kings xi.–xvii., relating to Israel, are important sections: xi. 1–xii. 21; xiv. 1–14, 17–22; xv. 1–7, 32–38, and xvi. 1–20, which refer to contemporary events in Judah. The accounts of the priestly revolution (xi. 1–20) and the subsequent repair of the Temple under Joash (xii. 4–16), were derived from early Judean sources. They, together with xvi. 10–18, which describes the altar erected by Ahaz, may have been based upon official records preserved in the Temple. Chapters xii. 17, 18; xiv. 8–14, 19, 20, 22; xv. 5, and xvi. 5–9 consist of concise political notices, gathered by the compiler, probably, from the state annals, and incorporated in his regular framework. With the exception of the short epitome inserted by the editor in xviii. 9–12, the rest of the Book of Kings, beginning with chapter xviii., is devoted entirely to Judah. The brief account of the invasion of Sennacherib in xviii. 13–16 was probably taken from the state records; while the more detailed narrative of the same, contained in xviii. 17 – xix. 37, and reproduced in Isaiah xxxvi. and xxxvii., in which Isaiah is the chief figure, is, like the stories of Elijah and Elisha,

from some prophetic historian living not long after the events recorded. Chapter xix. 21–31 preserves a short prophecy, practically as it fell from the lips of Isaiah. Chapter xx. 1–19 is also a prophetic narrative, evidently of still later date than the one contained in xviii. 17 – xix. 37. Chapter xxi., which treats of the reigns of Manasseh and Amon, contains some definite historical data (verses 3–7), although it consists mainly of the comments of the compiler. The narrative in Kings is supplemented by a few additional facts which have been preserved by the chronicler in the corresponding chapters (II. Chron. xxiii.–xxxiii.) of his work.

110. The Assyrian period of Judah's history is illuminated, at its most important crises, by the sermons of its greatest statesman-prophet. They treat every side of the nation's life, and consequently render this epoch one of the best known of Hebrew history. The prophecies of Isaiah, however, are not arranged in chronological order. With the aid of an occasional superscription and the testimony of internal evidence, it is possible to date those relating to Judah with comparative certainty. His call, recorded in chapter vi., was during the last year of Uzziah, between 740 and 737 B.C. Chapters ii. 5 – iv. 1 contain prophecies delivered about 735 B.C., during the reign of the weak Ahaz (iii. 12), and before the loss of Elath (ii. 16) to the Arameans in 734 B.C. To the same year belong the series of sermons preserved in v. 1–25; ix. 8 – x. 4 and v. 26–30, which distantly reflect the coming Aramean-Ephraimitish war. The addresses in vii. 1 – ix. 7, and xvii. 1–11 were delivered in 734 B.C., when these storm clouds from the north were

hovering over Judah. Chapter i. belongs either to this time, when the land was overrun by Arameans, Edomites, and Philistines, or to the even darker days of 701 B. C. The opening words of chapter xxviii., found in verses 1–6, were uttered shortly before the fall of Samaria in 722 B. C. The short prophecy in chapter xx. indicates Isaiah's attitude toward the uprising which called Sargon to Palestine in 711 B. C. Isaiah's activity reached its height in connection with the great rebellion against Assyria, which resulted in the invasion of Sennacherib in 701 B. C. The events recorded in the historical sections, xxxviii. and xxxix., belong to the years immediately preceding that crisis; the narratives themselves were taken from II. Kings. The short passage xiv. 29–32 reflects the exultation of the people of Palestine on hearing of the death of their oppressor Sargon in 705 B. C. As early as 703 B. C. the leaders of Judah began plotting, thereby arousing Isaiah to utter the words of warning preserved in xxviii. 7 – xxix. 24. Chapters xxx.–xxxii. and xxii. 15–25 come from a later period, probably 702 B. C., when alliances were being openly made with Egypt. To the year of the invasion itself, when the armies of Sennacherib were on the march toward Palestine, belong the sermons in x. 5 – xi. 9; xiv. 24–27. In xvii. 12–14 the city is about to be besieged; chapter xviii. pictures graphically the terror of the Ethiopians at this time, and xxii. 1–14 the confusion within Jerusalem and the wild rejoicing when the siege was raised. The historical sections xxxvi. and xxxvii., which record the final deliverance of the city, were, like xxxviii. and xxxix., taken from II. Kings. The remaining portions of the book either relate to foreign nations or else are from other hands, as is demonstrated by their style and contents.

111. The prophecies of Micah, a younger contemporary of Isaiah, deal especially with the social conditions in Judah. Chapters i.-iii., with the exception of ii. 12, 13, treat of the same general themes. The references in i. 1-7 to the impending fall of Samaria establish their date at a little before 722 B. C. Chapters iv. and v., if from Micah, may be assigned to the days of confusion and terror which attended the invasion of Sennacherib in 701 B. C. The most satisfactory historical background for vi. 1-vii. 6 is the reactionary reign of Manasseh. The style and thought of the remainder of chapter vii. is so different from that which precedes that its date and authorship are exceedingly uncertain.

112. Judah as well as Israel is frequently mentioned in the Assyrian inscriptions. In addition to the annals already referred to (sect. 57), those of Sennacherib contain a full account of the movements of this mighty conqueror, and especially the steps in his great western campaign of 701 B. C. The tribute lists of Esarhaddon and Ashurbanipal also afford valuable information respecting political conditions during the reign of Manasseh, which is passed over with such brief mention by the biblical historians.

113. The chronology of this period presents exceedingly intricate problems, arising from the conflicting testimony of the biblical data. The Assyrian chronology fixes two dates: (1) the accession of Athaliah to the throne of Judah after the slaughter of Azariah by Jehu in 842 B. C.; and (2) the invasion of Judah by Pekah and Rezon in 735-734 B. C., when Ahaz was

on the throne. We also know that Azariah (Uzziah) of Judah was defeated by Tiglath-Pileser III. in 740-738 B. C. Allowing only two or three years for the independent reign of Jotham, the year 735 B. C. is established approximately as the date of the accession of Ahaz. According to the chronological system of the compiler of Kings, a total of one hundred and forty-three (Athaliah, 6; Joash, 40; Amaziah, 29; Azariah, 52; Jotham, 16) years is assigned to the period of one hundred and seven years which intervened between the beginnings of the reigns of Athaliah and Ahaz, giving a discrepancy of thirty-six years. The six years of Athaliah and the forty of Joash seem to be well established. Amaziah's attack upon Jehoash of Israel (II. Kings xiv. 8-14) indicates that they were contemporaries. It probably occurred near the close of the reign of Jehoash, when he had recovered from the disastrous wars with Damascus. It has also been conjectured with reason that Amaziah's death at the hands of a conspiracy (II. Kings xiv. 19) was the result of his defeat. From these inferences, 782 B. C. may be accepted as the date of his death, giving him a reign of sixteen instead of twenty-nine years. The remaining twenty-three years must be deducted from the reigns of Azariah (Uzziah) and Jotham. Since Azariah was a leper, his son ruled as regent (II. Kings xv. 5). This accounts in part for the variation in the reckoning of the compiler, since he would give the full number of years during which each reigned. It is obvious that whatever system of dates is adopted for the first part of this period, they must be regarded as only approximate. In the chronological chart the system of Kamphausen has been generally followed.

114. The most perplexing although not the most important question in connection with the remainder of the period is the date of the accession of Hezekiah. Two distinct series of data point, the one to 715, and the other to 725 B. C. The date (715 B. C.) accepted by the majority of German scholars rests primarily upon II. Kings xviii. 13, which states that Sennacherib's invasion of 701 B. C. fell in the fourteenth year of Hezekiah. This seems to be confirmed by II. Kings xx. 1-6, which associates Hezekiah's sickness with Sennacherib's invasion, and contains the prophecy that the king would survive his illness fifteen years (verse 6). It may, however, have been from this statement that the author of II. Kings xviii. 13, knowing that Hezekiah reigned in all twenty-nine years, drew the inference that the great invasion was in his fourteenth ($29 - 15 = 14$) year. Furthermore, it is distinctly stated (II. Kings xx. 12; Isa. xxxix. 1) that Merodach-Baladan of Babylon sent an embassy to Hezekiah during his illness. From the inscriptions of Sennacherib it is established that the power of Merodach-Baladan was broken in 704-3 B. C. The date of his embassy, therefore, and of Hezekiah's illness (in his fourteenth year) must have been still earlier, so that the accession of the latter could not have been as late as 715 B. C.

115. On the other hand, II. Kings xviii. 10 definitely states that Samaria was taken in the sixth year of Hezekiah. Addition of the years assigned to Hezekiah and the kings of Judah who succeeded him before the fall of Jerusalem in 586 B. C. fixes the beginning of his reign at 725 B. C., which is in practical agreement with the passage just cited. There are good grounds for regarding the number of years

DATE OF HEZEKIAH'S ACCESSION 119

assigned to these kings as substantially correct, since their reigns were not so far removed from the age of the compiler as were those of the earlier days. Under Ahaz, Hezekiah, and Manasseh, also, the influence of Assyria became paramount in Judah, as was manifested in the introduction of a new style of altar (II. Kings xvi. 10), and eastern customs (Isa. ii. 6), and, as a result, from this time on a more exact system of reckoning time seems to have been adopted. Jeremiah and Ezekiel regularly date their prophecies according to the year of the reigning king. Furthermore, when we are able by these other sources to verify the number of years assigned by the compiler to the later kings, we find them substantially correct. The reference in Jeremiah xxvi. 18, which states positively that the sermons of Micah were delivered during the days of Hezekiah, obviously points to 725 rather than 715 B. C., since this prophecy foretells the fate of Samaria (722 B. C.). Whichever date be accepted, the sixteen years assigned to the reign of Ahaz cannot stand. Perhaps the most serious objection to the earlier date is its inconsistency with the ages of Ahaz and Hezekiah at their accession. Ahaz could not have died when only thirty years old and left a son aged twenty-five. These, however, are details which posterity would be least likely to record, and respecting which the compiler has elsewhere shown that he was dependent upon conjecture. In the light of all the evidence, therefore, 725 B. C. is the more probable date for the accession of Hezekiah.

II

FROM ATHALIAH TO AHAZ

116. THE revolution of Jehu, which included the slaughter of Ahaziah of Judah and thereby gave the unscrupulous Athaliah an opportunity to seize the throne, was followed, six years later, by a counter revolution in the southern kingdom, likewise inspired by the more zealous champions of the worship of Jehovah. It is significant that the one who planned it was not a prophet, but Jehoiada, the priest of the temple of Jehovah, where Joash, the youthful son of the murdered Ahaziah, had been hidden by his aunt from Athaliah's destructive hand. The details of the conspiracy were carefully prepared, and the captains of the royal guard previously pledged to co-operate. The *coup d'état* took place on a Sabbath day. The guard, who regularly assumed charge of the Temple on that day, were posted at such points as commanded the passage from the palace and the other entrances to the sanctuary. The Temple guard, which was ordinarily relieved from duty on the Sabbath, was ordered to remain and protect the person of the young king. The prestige of the house of David gave force to the movement. In the hands of the guard were placed the spears and shields which had been won

from their foes by the great conqueror, whose offspring they were about to restore to the throne of his ancestors. When all was ready, the little Joash (or Jehoash) was led forth and duly anointed king. The cry of guard and people, "Let the king live," was the first intimation which Athaliah received of the conspiracy. Her exclamation of "Treason" aroused no response. She was slain within the palace at the command of Jehoiada, who virtually acted as regent during the boyhood of the new ruler.

117. A solemn covenant was then made between Jehovah and the people "that they should be the Lord's people." Elijah's words of protest against the toleration of Baal worship found a response in Judah as well as in Israel. Under the influence of the reaction, and doubtless at the instigation of the priest, Jehoiada, the people went to the temple of Baal, which had been allowed to flourish undisturbed beneath the shadows of the capital, and tore it down, levelling altars and images, and slaying its priest, Mattan, in the midst of the ruin to make the desecration complete. Thus, with little bloodshed, was consummated the important revolution whereby the family of David was restored to the throne of Judah, and Baalism placed under a ban.

118. A century and a half had elapsed since the building of Solomon's Temple; and consequently the demand for repairs was imperative. While the reigning family of Judah was coquetting with the house of Ahab and countenancing a temple of Baal at Jerusalem, the temple of Jehovah was neglected. Joash, however, who had been raised to the throne by a priestly revolution, was under obligation to repay the

debt thus incurred. He accordingly turned over to the priests the regular religious tax, as well as the voluntary offerings, with the understanding that they were, with the proceeds, to see that the necessary repairs were completed. Twenty-three years passed, however, and nothing was done. When, at last, they were called to account by the king, Jehoiada introduced the simple but effective device of placing at the right side of the entrance of the Temple a chest with a hole in the lid into which the priests who guarded the door cast the offerings of the people. As the money accumulated, it was taken from thence by the priest and royal secretary and paid directly to the workmen. In this way the structure of the Temple was rescued from decay.

119. The long reign of Joash was further characterized by a threatened invasion led by the ambitious king of Damascus, Hazael, who not only overran Israel, but also attacked the Philistine town of Gath, which he captured and destroyed so effectually that it henceforth disappeared from the list of the Philistine Pentapolis. Jerusalem was the next place toward which he turned for plunder. Joash, however, anticipated attack, and saved his capital by turning over to Hazael the accumulated treasures of the Temple and palace. The latter part of his reign was further darkened by a conspiracy among his servants, who for some unknown cause slew him at the house of Millo.

120. The hereditary principle was so strong in Judah that Amaziah, his son, succeeded Joash without serious opposition. As soon as he became the real master of his realm, he avenged the death of his father by slaying his murderers. For the first time (com-

pare Josh. vii. 24-26; II. Sam. xxi.; II. Kings ix. 26) the milder custom, which finds expression in Deuteronomy xxiv. 16, of not visiting upon the innocent offspring the crimes of the parent, was observed. The act represented such a marked advance toward civilization that it justly commanded the especial attention of the writer of II. Kings xiv. 6. Amaziah's attitude toward the national religion was, like that of his father, exceedingly friendly.

121. During the earlier part of the Assyrian period of Judean history the smaller and more protected Hebrew kingdom felt the influence of the great empire on the Tigris only indirectly. When the power of Damascus was broken, it improved the opportunity, as did Israel, to extend its boundaries. Since the days of Jehoram (sect. 45), the Edomites had maintained their independence. Amaziah invaded their land, and fought a successful battle in the Valley of Salt, to the south of the Dead Sea, in which a large number of the Edomites were slain. Sela ("The Rock," better known by its later Greek name Petra) was captured, and its name changed to Joktheel, as long as it remained under the sway of Judah. Amaziah's conquests appear to have extended southward to Elath, on the Red Sea (II. Kings xiv. 22); but the Edomites still retained the eastern portion of their territory. Amos later predicted the coming destruction of Teman and Bozrah, which in his day were the chief Edomite cities (i. 12). The kings of Edom figure frequently among the princes of Palestine, who subsequently paid tribute to the conquering monarchs of Assyria, and there is no evidence that they were subject to Judah.

122. Elated by his victory over the Edomites, Amaziah sent his fatal challenge to Joash of Israel (sect. 75). Although the power of the northern kingdom had been broken by its long wars with Damascus, it was rapidly recovering, and its resources far exceeded those of Judah. Joash, therefore, showed a fraternal consideration for his cousins of the south in endeavoring to persuade Amaziah to desist from his foolhardy enterprise; but the Judean king refused to listen, and learned his error when, at Bethshemesh, he was deserted by his army and found himself the captive of the king of Israel. A long section of the wall of Jerusalem was torn down, the Temple and palace were despoiled of their treasures, and hostages taken. Like his father, Amaziah fell a victim to a conspiracy. The cause was probably the discontent aroused by the disastrous results of his rash attack upon Israel. Recognizing his danger, he fled from Jerusalem to the border town of Lachish, whither his assassins pursued and where they slew him. He was, however, accorded a burial in the royal tombs, and his son regularly succeeded him.

123. The youth of sixteen who was thus raised to the throne of Judah possessed the energy of his father, and in addition a prudence and organizing ability which made his reign the most glorious since the division of the kingdoms. His official name appears to have been Azariah. This is the one by which he is generally known in the Book of Kings, and also on the Assyrian monuments, while in the prophecies and Chronicles (excepting I. Chron. iii. 13) he is called Uzziah. The latter may have been the name by which he was familiarly known among his people, but, by later genera-

tions, it was shortened still further to Uzza (II. Kings xxi. 18, 26). He was afflicted by leprosy, and so, in accordance with the inexorable Hebrew custom, which made no exception even for a king, was obliged to dwell in his separate palace. His son, Jotham, assumed charge of the court, and discharged the public duties of the king as judge of the realm.

124. The Book of Kings is as silent respecting the long and important reign of Azariah (Uzziah) as it is concerning that of his contemporary, Jeroboam II. of Israel. The chronicler, however, has preserved an account of his military successes which may be regarded as historical. While Israel was extending its boundaries in the north and east, Judah was pushing in the opposite directions. The territory of the Philistines, whose power had been broken by the Arameans (sect. 119), was invaded and several of their cities captured. Hebrew colonies were settled in the lands thus annexed. The prophet Micah, who came from Moresheth, a little town tributary to Gath (Micah i. 1, 14), was probably a descendant of these colonists. Some of the towns mentioned in his opening prophecy (i. 10-16) may have been those founded by Azariah (Uzziah) at this time. Elath, the Edomite town on the Red Sea, which had been the port from which Hebrew ships in the earlier days went forth to engage in trade with Arabia and India, was rebuilt. The revival of commerce, therefore, explains in part the prosperity of the period. Azariah's wars against the Arabian tribes were presumably to protect his merchants and to secure an undisturbed passage to the port on the Red Sea. The series of building enterprises attributed to him by the chronicler is quite

in accord with his character. The walls of Jerusalem were rebuilt and provided with towers; the army also was thoroughly organized; cisterns were dug to collect and retain the winter rains; and watch-towers were constructed in the wilderness for the protection of the herds of cattle which belonged to the king. In the uplands he had many fields, carefully tilled by husbandmen and vinedressers, since he was a patron and lover of agriculture.

125. From two fragmentary inscriptions of Tiglath-Pileser III., we learn that the influence of this strong Judean king was felt throughout the Palestinian world. Jeroboam II. died about 740 B. C., and Israel quickly fell into disorder (sect. 96). This perhaps explains why in 739 or 738 B. C., Azariah (Uzziah) was recognized as the leader of the coalition of Syrian states which attempted to check the advance of Assyria in the north. The effort, however, was in vain. The cities of Hamath were subjugated by Tiglath-Pileser. Judah escaped immediate invasion simply because its territory was far removed from the scene of its defeat. The reference to Azariah (Uzziah) in the Assyrian inscriptions also indicates that he survived nearly as long as his son Jotham, whose independent reign could not have extended beyond two or three years at the longest (compare sect. 113). He continued the policy of his father, and distinguished his rule by building the upper gate of the Temple. His last year was darkened by the threatened invasion of the allied kings of Israel and Damascus, and he died, leaving this danger as an unpleasant heritage to his son Ahaz.

III

THE CRISIS OF 734 B. C.

126. THE occasion of the invasion of Judah by its two northern neighbors was, as has been indicated (sect. 99), their determination to force the southern kingdom to unite with them in a revolt against Assyria. The kings of Judah had measured their strength with this world-power only a few years before, and were loath to venture another experiment. The northern allies, however, were insistent. The armies of Damascus captured the port of Elath, expelling the Judeans, and thus cut off the source of the nation's wealth. When Ahaz still refused to join the coalition, Pekah of Israel and Rezon of Damascus made preparations to march upon Jerusalem, depose its unpatriotic king, and install a certain son of Tabeel in his place. Undoubtedly within the city itself there was a strong party favorable to the coalition (Isa. viii. 6). The energetic foe might appear without the walls at any time. According to the chronicler (II. Chron. xxviii. 5-18), the armies of Judah had already suffered an overwhelming defeat at the hands of the confederates. Edomites and Philistines had also taken advantage of the weakness of their old enemy and master, to devastate and overrun its southern towns. Well may Isaiah's words, preserved in chapter i. 7, 8, have been uttered at this time "Your country is desolate; your cities are burned with fire; your land, strangers are devouring it in your presence, and it is desolate, as the overthrow of strangers. And the daughter of Zion is left as a booth in a vineyard, as a lodge in a garden of cucumbers, as a besieged city." Hearts of king and people were moved " as the trees of the forest are moved with the wind " (Isa. vii. 2). The future of Judah depended upon the policy which should then be adopted.

127. The crisis brought into prominence two men of widely different character. Ahaz, the king, possessed all of the faults with few of the virtues of the descendants of David. He was superficial, cowardly, superstitious, and selfishly indifferent to the welfare of his nation. In him we recognize a characteristic product of the luxurious reign of Azariah (Uzziah). He was more at home in the harem than on the throne. His youth and inexperience alone palliate his faults.

128. Isaiah, the prophet, was at this time also a young man. His ability and the influence which he exerted in the state strengthen the testimony of tradition, which maintains that he was closely connected with the royal family. He had grown up at Jerusalem, familiar with the life of the court, and also with that broader field of Semitic politics into which Judah was then entering. About the time of his birth the remarkable mission of the Judean Amos to Israel occurred. The ministry of Hosea had just been completed. The grave social and religious problems with which they had grappled were already present in Judah. Related as intimately as was the

smaller Hebrew kingdom to the greater, the revolutionizing messages of these prophets were undoubtedly familiar to the more enlightened men in the south. Isaiah's prophecies indicate that as a young man he was acquainted with these great teachers of the north, if not personally, at least through their written or popularly reported sermons.

129. As his eyes were divinely opened to a broader and deeper conception of Jehovah and a truer appreciation of conditions within and without Judah, the conviction deepened that some one must undertake the task, unpleasant as it would necessarily be, of proclaiming the new truth to the nation. Four or five years before the crisis of 734 B. C., this conviction culminated in a definite and personal call for him to be a prophet. The day and hour were indelibly fixed in his memory (vi. 1). As his spiritual vision was clarified under the influence of the Spirit of the Highest, he was enabled to see the real instead of the symbol. In place of the Temple, the Ark and the cherubim, he beheld the God of perfect holiness, seated upon his throne. In the presence of the Holy One he realized his own sinfulness and that of his nation with a vividness unequalled before, perhaps, in the history of man. The realization of the awful contrast presented the need which was the occasion of his call. His own symbolic cleansing was an earnest of the free forgiveness which would always follow the cry of penitence. The voice of duty was plainly recognized as the voice of God calling for a messenger to send to his people. Unhesitatingly Isaiah offered himself and was accepted. Henceforth his life-work was to preach truth to a nation which turned toward it only a deaf ear; and,

like Hosea, he was destined to see the cities of his beloved land laid waste and devastated simply because of this stubborn refusal to listen.

130. At first Isaiah confined himself to denunciation of the social and religious evils which had crept into the life of Judah (sect. 110); but the needs of the situation in 734 B. C. called him to political activity. Accompanied by his little son, Shear-Jashub, whose name ("A remnant shall return") was in itself a prophecy of hope, he met Ahaz one day near the conduit, which probably led from the pool within the city, where was stored the water which issued from the present Virgin's Fount, to a point without the walls. The presence of the king at this place suggests that he was making preparations for the impending siege. Isaiah's words, addressed directly to him, were calculated to inspire confidence, and may be briefly paraphrased: "Be watchful, O king, and commit yourself to no rash policy; be not terrified by the threatening foes, for their show of power is like the last fierce flame which blazes up before a firebrand burns out completely. Surely you are not afraid of that conspirator, Pekah, who has incited Israel to make this attack, nor of his ally, Rezon. It is Jehovah's will that their plans shall be overturned. Israel itself, before many years, shall go down to its ruin; therefore you have no cause for fear; but if you do not believe, surely you shall not be established."

131. Knowing, perhaps, that Ahaz was already planning ignominiously to purchase present deliverance by selling his freedom to Assyria, the common foe, the prophet waited to see whether or not he would heed his words. Perceiving that they had made no impres-

sion, he demanded, "Ask thee a sign of the Lord, thy God; ask it either in the depth, or in the height above;" but he was speaking to deaf ears. Unwilling to be convinced, Ahaz replied, "I will not ask, neither will I tempt the Lord." Indignantly Isaiah turned upon the hypocritical king and his faithless princes, who were "a weariness to man and God" alike, and, after rebuking them, announced unasked his mysterious sign: "A young woman shall bear a son; amidst destitution shall he grow up, but before he shall attain to the years of discretion the territory of these foes whom you now fear shall be desolate." The name of the child, Immanu-El (God-with-us), contained a promise of that perfect era toward which the prophet, surrounded as he was by so much that was imperfect, confidently looked; but whether the child was the ideal king of his later prophecies, his own offspring, a son of King Ahaz, or any child that might be born at that time, it is clear, in the light of the context, that the allusion to his birth was intended primarily as a sign that Israel and Damascus, and Judah also, would soon be devastated by the foreign conqueror. Casting aside symbolism, in the following verses Isaiah plainly declares to Ahaz that the nation whose favor he is courting will prove the instrument whereby Jehovah will bring a desolating judgment upon Judah, and that his land is about to become the scene of the great contest between the world powers, Egypt and Assyria.

132. Isaiah's utterances at this time reveal the clearness and depth of his political insight. He not only correctly estimated the relative strength of the nations with which Judah must deal, but anticipated their future movements. His policy of holding

aloof from all foreign entanglements was dictated by reason as well as by faith in Jehovah; for union with Pekah and Rezon would be suicide; and alliance with Assyria only hastened the time when the yoke of the rapacious conqueror should rest upon the neck of little Judah. Ahaz, however, rejected the advice of his wisest counsellor, and hastened to become the vassal of his deadliest foe. "I am thy servant and thy son," was the fawning message which he sent to Tiglath-Pileser. Temple and palace were despoiled of their treasures to swell the present wherewith Judah's subjection was purchased.

133. Treated with scorn by king and princes, Isaiah turned to the people. No means were left untried to impress his message upon his countrymen. On a great tablet he inscribed the significant motto, "Swift spoil, speedy prey," and placed it in a conspicuous place where all could read it. Imitating the example of Hosea (Hosea i. 4–9), he gave as a name to a child who was born to him at that time the same alarming words which proclaimed the speedy devastation of Samaria and Damascus by the hands of the Assyrians (viii. 3, 4). Thus he endeavored to allay the terror inspired by the cry of "conspiracy" which had rung throughout the city when the news had come of the advance of the northern confederates, and to arouse instead a genuine trust in Jehovah (Isa. viii. 12). The faith of the masses, however, proved no stronger than that of their king and princes. In their fright they forgot Jehovah, and resorted unto those who had "familiar spirits and unto the wizards that chirp and that mutter" (viii. 19). Only his few faithful disciples, "the children whom the Lord had given him," were

ready to wait for Jehovah, who had for the time being "hidden his face from the house of Jacob" (viii. 17, 18). In them he recognized the true hope of Judah; they were "for signs and wonders in Israel." Henceforth he devoted himself to instructing them (viii. 16).

134. Tiglath-Pileser III. advanced with such rapidity that the states of Palestine, which had been wasting their energies in civil war, were unable to make a united defence (compare sect. 99). As Isaiah had predicted, nation after nation was broken in pieces. Torrents of blood flowed from one end of Syria to the other. Pekah of Israel was among the first to fall. Judah alone enjoyed the immunity from attack which it had purchased at so great a cost. Among the vassal princes who assembled at Damascus to do homage to the conqueror was Ahaz of Judah. Deterred by no strong religious principles, he caused the old brazen altar which stood before the Temple at Jerusalem to be moved to the north, and on its site he reared a new altar after the style of one which he had seen in Damascus. To gratify his Assyrian master still further, he commanded that all the regular offerings should be burnt upon this foreign altar. Other innovations were introduced into the Temple, presumably with the same object. Even within their most sacred sanctuary, the Judeans were not allowed to forget that their honor and independence had been forfeited by their cowardly king.

IV

SOCIETY AND RELIGION IN JUDAH

135. FOR the first century and a half after the division of the Hebrew empire, society in Judah reverted to the simplicity of the earlier days. Jerusalem, perched on a barren plateau, surrounded by dry ravines and limestone hills, was the insignificant capital of a little nation of herdsmen and vinedressers. Their poverty and natural seclusion rendered important social transformations impossible. During the reign of Azariah (Uzziah), however, the smaller Hebrew kingdom was exposed to the same temptations to which the larger and richer northern state had long been subjected. The prolonged and prosperous reign of this able king not only extended Judah's boundaries and influence, but also brought wealth and peace unknown since the days of Solomon. The capture of the Edomite towns of Sela and Elath opened the way for commerce with Arabia and India. The approach of Assyria introduced the states of Palestine to the greater world without, and inspired in them the material ambitions by which this great people were at this time dominated.

136. The same forces, therefore, which revolutionized society in Israel, were actively at work in Judah.

They began to be felt most strongly during the reigns of Jotham, Ahaz, and Hezekiah. We might suspect that Amos magnified the social evils of Israel, did not the royal prophet Isaiah and his contemporary, Micah, picture those of Judah in still darker colors. Danger from without always led the prophets to study conditions within the state more closely, just as to-day extra sanitary precautions are taken when a dread pestilence threatens. Consequently the social sermons of the prophets were delivered in connection with the crises of their nation.

137. The earliest public addresses of Isaiah with which we are familiar were upon social themes, and belong to the troublesome days preceding the invasion of 734 B.C. The one preserved in chapter v. may be regarded as typical. Like Amos, with consummate skill he gains the hearing of his audience before pronouncing their condemnation. Accordingly he asks permission to sing to them a song. His words are cast in the light, tripping metre of the vineyard ditty, so agreeable to the ears of a people whose chief occupation was the culture of the vine; the theme also was a vineyard established by a dear friend. Briefly he recounts how a fair site was selected, the ground prepared and no pains spared to make it perfect in every detail; but, alas, its fruit! It has only wild grapes. "Is it not just, O Judeans, to destroy utterly this vineyard?" While their heads are still nodding in ready assent, like a flash comes the application: "Israel is the vineyard, carefully planted by Jehovah. Judah is his favorite vine. Are the fruits justice and righteousness? No; only oppression and the cry of the wronged." Not content with general denunciations,

the prophet proceeds to point out the most heinous crimes: "Woe unto them that join house to house, that lay field to field, till there be no room, and ye be made to dwell alone in the midst of the land." So vivid is the picture that one can see the rich nobles gradually driving out their poorer neighbors from their little ancestral possessions, that they may add acre after acre to their huge estates. Micah a few years later echoed the same protest: "Woe to them that devise iniquity and work evil upon their beds! When the morning is light they practise it, because it is in the power of their hand; and they covet fields, and seize them; and houses, and take them away; and they oppress a man and his house, even a man and his heritage" (ii. 1, 2). Both prophets recognized that this process was rapidly reducing the independent freedmen to servitude and thereby destroying the middle class in Judah.

138. Again Isaiah pronounced a woe upon those who make drinking and feasting the chief end of their existence. He realized that the whole community suffered from this wanton waste: "Therefore my people are gone into captivity, for lack of knowledge; and their honorable men are famished, and their multitude are parched with thirst." So great was his abhorrence of the intemperance in Judah that the prophet utters in the same sermon (verses 22, 23) another contemptuous woe against those "mighty to drink wine and men of strength to mingle strong drink."

139. The prophets of Judah, like those of Israel, recognized that the rulers were chiefly to blame for the awful social corruption. Micah, who regarded them,

as did Amos, from the point of view of the masses, declared that they were cannibals "who tear the flesh of the people from their bones and eat it" (iii. 2, 3). Their greed and rapacity knew no limit. Like highway robbers they pounced upon the passer-by and stripped off his robe (ii. 8). Helpless women and children were their especial prey (ii. 9). Under the name of justice, decisions were given to the one who offered the highest bribe (iii. 11). Isaiah, the royal prophet, repeatedly denounced them in language equally strong: "They that lead Judah cause it to err. They spoil the poor in their houses and crush my people" (iii. 14, 15). "The princes are companions of thieves; everyone loveth gifts and hath no regard for the cause of the widow and fatherless" (i. 23). The women of Judah also were ruled by a passion, not for gratifying their appetites, as were those of Israel, but for show and adornment, which was leading them on to commit the most cruel excesses (Isa. iii. 16, 17). None of the social evils to which an Oriental state is peculiarly subject were lacking in Judah. The little kingdom was poorly prepared to weather the terrific storms which were about to sweep over it; for, according to the testimony of its acutest statesman, "from the sole of the foot even unto the head, there was no soundness in it" (Isa. i. 6).

140. Since it bore such evil fruits, it may be inferred that the religion of Judah was little better than that of Israel. The few historical references confirm the truth of this inference. Until the political revolution instigated by Jehoiada (sect. 118) overthrew the temple and worship of the Tyrian Baal, they appear to have been tolerated without open opposition. The

revolution itself represented not so much an advance as a return to ideas and forms already generally accepted. The religious history of Judah, therefore, during the first century of the Assyrian period is marked by little appreciable progress. The popular conceptions of Jehovah and the forms with which he was worshipped were the same as in the earlier days. The compiler of Kings, viewing the history from a later period, considered it a sin that "the high places were not taken away; the people still sacrificed and burnt incense in the high places." But the age saw in it nothing wrong; for the sanctuary at Jerusalem had not yet attained its commanding prestige.

141. Under the influence of the Canaanitish cult, the people still worshipped trees as symbols of life, and indulged in the debasing practices associated therewith (Isa. i. 29); but Baalism never proved as seductive to the Judeans as to the Israelites, whose territory was largely agricultural. Instead, they appear to have retained many of the primitive superstitions, inherited from their nomadic past, and conserved by their constant contact with the tribes of the desert. Into the reign of Hezekiah the masses continued to worship a brazen serpent which was associated with the name of Moses (II. Kings xviii. 4). Isaiah complained that "Their land also is full of idols; they worship the work of their own hands, that which their own fingers have made" (ii. 8). Idols of silver and of gold, probably corresponding to the teraphim, or family idols, frequently referred to in the earlier times (I. sects. 69, 167), seem to have been commonly found in the possession of private individuals as well as in the public sanctuaries (Isa. ii. 20).

FALSE PRIESTS AND PROPHETS

142. Their unjustifiable appropriation of the funds intended for the repair of the Temple indicates that the priests of the royal sanctuary during the days of Joash, when the greatest purity might have been expected, were little better than those who ministered at the northern shrines. Micah, with his usual bluntness, declared that the priests of his day taught for hire (iii. 11). The official prophets he condemns still more severely; not only do they "divine for money" (iii. 11), but "they even prepare war against the one who putteth not into their mouths" (iii. 5). Deuteronomy xviii. 9–22 declares that one of the missions of the true prophet is to take the place of the diviners, augurs, enchanters, sorcerers, charmers, consulters with familiar spirits, wizards, and necromancers to whom the people were wont to resort. Isaiah refers to these false religious guides as being very common in his day, and speaks sorrowfully of those who go to consult them (viii. 19; xxix. 4; iii. 3). Both Isaiah (iii. 2) and Micah (iii. 7) associate them with the regular prophets of Jehovah. Their references imply that the people considered them to be as reputable and important members of the community as the judge, the priest, the military captain, and the counsellor.

143. The same fundamental errors characterized the popular religion of both Judah and Israel. A formal, ceremonial service was regarded as sufficient, and morality as almost non-essential (Isa. i. 10–17; Micah vi. 6–8). Jehovah ever remained the tribal god of Judah; but this did not deter the ordinary citizen, nor such a king as Ahaz, from "making his son to pass through the fire according to the abominations of the heathen" (II. Kings xvi. 3), and from

freely adopting foreign customs (Isa. ii. 6), and even from paying homage to the deities of the surrounding nations (Micah i. 13). Reformations more fundamental than that which is attributed to Hezekiah by the author of Kings (II. Kings xviii. 4), and which would transform the formal ceremonial into an ethical and spiritual religion, were required, before the faith of Judah would be prepared to meet the supreme test which awaited it. An understanding of the prevailing religious conditions and ideas alone furnishes the basis for an adequate appreciation of the marvellous degree of spiritual enlightenment which was vouchsafed to the prophets who proclaimed the true God to their nation. The striking contrast between popular and prophetic faith is explained only as we recognize the patent fact that "Jehovah had spoken to his servants."

V

THE GREAT INVASION OF SENNACHERIB

144. THE fall of Samaria in 722 B. C. made an impression upon Judah which was not soon forgotten. This was deepened, when two years later Sargon met and signally defeated an Egyptian army under Shabaka, near Raphia, on the borders of the land of the Nile. The Judeans were thus enabled to learn by observation, instead of by bitter experience, that Assyria was practically invincible. For two decades they profited by this knowledge, paid tribute to Sargon, and as a result enjoyed peace and prosperity. The public treasury, depleted by Ahaz, was again filled (II. Kings xx. 13), and the Philistine territory, as far as Gaza, was conquered (II. Kings xviii. 8). To this period must also be assigned the construction by Hezekiah of the pool and conduit whereby water was brought within the city to insure a supply in time of siege (II. Kings xx. 20). This work may be identified with the rock-cut tunnel, discovered in 1880, which conducts the water which flows from the present Virgin's Fount, south of the Temple hill, to the pool of Siloam, which was within the ancient city walls, and within which was found the ancient Hebrew inscription describing the process of construction.

Hezekiah also figures as a patron of literature. The collection of proverbs preserved in chapters xxv.-xxix. of the Book of Proverbs, according to the superscription (xxv. 1), "were copied out" by his scribes.

145. The petty states of Palestine bore with impatience the galling yoke of Assyria. The masses in time forgot the lessons which they had learned and listened only too readily to Egypt, which, consistently with its usual policy, was endeavoring to stir up rebellion among the vassals of its powerful rival. Consequently in most of the cities of Syria there arose a party who, relying upon the aid of Egypt, were eager to try their chances in a revolt. In 711 B. C. this element gained the ascendency in the Philistine town of Ashdod, and induced it to refuse the usual tribute. Gath was drawn into the rebellion, and a strong party in Judah favored union with the rebels. To avert the danger, Isaiah employed extreme measures to bring his countrymen to their senses and keep them true to their pledges to Assyria. Taking off his outer garment, with bare feet, in the significant garb of a captive, he went about Jerusalem for three years "as a sign and a wonder upon Egypt and Ethiopia" (Isa. xx. 3). His words and action dissipated the popular illusion respecting Egypt's strength sufficiently to save Judah from becoming fatally involved. Sargon, recognizing the danger of a general uprising, advanced with lightning rapidity (as he assures us in his inscriptions), not even waiting to collect his entire army. Ashdod found itself deserted by its allies; the rebel king fled to Egypt, and the rigors of conquest were visited upon the inhabitants. The tribute and presents of Judah, Edom, and Moab, "who were plotting revolt

and treason" (Sargon Cyl. Inscp. 29) were accepted, and peace was established in Palestine.

146. While Sargon lived, the subject peoples remained quiet; but his assassination in 705 B. C. was a cause of wild rejoicing (Isa. xiv. 29), and became the occasion of a widespread uprising. Merodach-Baladan, the king of Babylon who had been overthrown and driven from his capital in 709 B. C., returned to head the revolt in the east. Outside of Babylonia, he induced the Elamites, certain Arameans of Mesopotamia, and Arabian tribes to unite with him. It was probably at this time that his ambassadors appeared in Jerusalem and were so cordially received by Hezekiah (II. Kings xx. 12–21; Isa. xxxix.). The readiness of the Judean king to show them all the treasures and equipment of his capital, and the indignant protest of Isaiah are explained when it becomes clear that their mission, although ostensibly to congratulate Hezekiah on his recovery from a severe illness, was in reality to induce him to join the grand coalition.

147. Isaiah, who in 734 B. C. had so strenuously opposed alliance with Assyria, now exerted all his influence to deter the leaders of his nation from taking the fatal steps. "In quietness and in confidence shall be your strength" (xxx. 15) was the keynote of all his teaching. The statesmen of Judah, however, were intoxicated with the spirit of revolt (Isa. xxviii. 7; xxx. 9). Prophets, seers, and wise men. with their siren songs, encouraged them in their wild course (xxix. 9–14). A mad recklessness took possession of all, and the baser elements, "the scornful men," ruled public opinion (xxviii. 14, 15). Isaiah's "precept

upon precept and line upon line," which had held Judah to a true course for thirty years, were rejected (xxviii. 9–13). In vain he declared that "out of the serpent's root shall come forth an adder," and with prophetic vision pointed out the "smoke that cometh out of the north" (xiv. 29, 31). The nations, however, could not believe that another conqueror like Sargon would rise in his stead. At first the anti-Assyrian party carried on their counsels in secret, fearing, doubtless, the opposition of Isaiah (xxix. 15); but at length Judah openly arrayed itself under the standard of revolt. Already this had been raised in the towns of Phœnicia and Philistia. Sidon in the north, and Ekron in the south were the leaders. Padi, the vassal king of Ekron, who remained faithful to his Assyrian master, was sent in chains to Jerusalem. Ambassadors were despatched to secure the aid of Tirhakah, the Ethiopian prince who had recently usurped the throne of Egypt. Isaiah pointed with scorn to "Egypt that helpeth in vain, and to no purpose; therefore, have I called her Rahab, that sitteth still" (xxx. 7). His charge against the leaders of Jerusalem, however, was not merely one of folly and shortsightedness. Their supreme mistake was that "they looked not unto the Holy One of Israel, neither sought the Lord;" instead, they placed their whole trust in their military equipment and "in the shadow of Egypt" (xxxi. 1; xxx. 1–4), forgetting that "the Egyptians were men and not God; and their horses flesh and not spirit" (xxxi. 3). From the first Isaiah took his stand upon the principle that Zion was inviolable, and declared that although the rulers of Judah should learn to their shame the folly of their

SENNACHERIB'S CONQUEST OF PALESTINE 145

plans, yet at the last Jehovah would deliver his holy city (xxix. 5-8; xxxi. 4-9).

148. Events soon demonstrated the truth of the prophet's position. Sennacherib, who succeeded Sargon, proved as active a general as his father. Until 702 B. C. he was occupied in suppressing the rebellion in the east. Merodach-Baladan was at last completely vanquished. Master of the east, Sennacherib turned his large army, now flushed with victory, toward Palestine. He found the rebels poorly organized. Without aiding one another, they each fell in turn an easy prey. His march lay along the coast of the Mediterranean. Sidon fell first, with its dependent towns. "Ethobal upon the royal throne, I placed over them, and the payment of the tribute of my lordship, every year without change, I laid upon him. Menahem of Samsimuruna [Samaria], Ethobal of Sidon, Mitinti of Ashdod, Buduilu of Ammon, Chemoshnadab of Moab, Malik-rammu of Edom (all the kings of the west-land) brought rich presents, heavy gifts together with merchandise before me, and kissed my feet," is the testimony of the conqueror (Taylor Prism, ii. 44-57). At the first blow, therefore, half the princes of Palestine hastened to submit. From Phœnicia, Sennacherib marched at once against the Philistine town of Askelon, capturing it, and thereby preventing a union between the rebels and their Egyptian allies. Thence he turned back against Ekron, which had led the uprising. While besieging this city he met, at the neighboring town of Eltekeh, an army sent by Tirhakah to the relief of Ekron. According to the Assyrian annals, the Egyptian troops experienced a signal defeat. They were certainly forced to retire, leaving Ekron and

Judah to their fate. Longer resistance was hopeless. The bodies of the rebellious princes of the Philistine city were impaled on stakes without its walls, and their supporters carried away into captivity, and the deposed king, Padi, restored to his throne.

149. The evils which were about to overtake his countrymen were due to the mistakes against which Isaiah had repeatedly warned them, yet he did not remain silent. As the gloom deepened, his prophecies of ultimate deliverance became more definite and certain. Even while the Assyrians were in the north he uttered the sublime address contained in x. 5–xi. 9: "Assyria is advancing," is the underlying thought, "crushing nations, and will yet bring woe to rebellious Judah; but it is only the rod wherewith Jehovah executes judgment. The proud king of Assyria, however, does not recognize this fact. In his arrogance he boasts that by the strength of his own hand he has conquered the world. Shall the ax boast itself against him that heweth therewith? The Assyrians shall be allowed to advance unopposed to the very walls of Jerusalem, and then Jehovah will suddenly arise and cast them down in utter ruin. As the danger increased, the prophet repeatedly proclaimed these stupendous truths (xiv. 24–27; xvii. 12–14). The basis of his predictions was the realization that the God of Judah was the Lord of hosts whose "hand is stretched out upon all the nations, and whose purpose none can disannul" (xiv. 27). That he would allow this arrogant monster of greed and cruelty to crush completely his chosen people was incredible.

150. While Isaiah was predicting his downfall, Sennacherib was completing the conquest of the Philistine

towns, and sending detachments of his army up the valleys of Judah (Isa. xxii. 7). Forty-six of its cities were captured. According to the conqueror, over two hundred thousand Jewish captives were dragged away, together with huge spoil, consisting of horses, mules, asses, camels, oxen, and innumerable sheep. The territory thus ravaged was divided between their old enemies, the kings of Ashdod, Ekron, and Gaza, to make the humiliation greater; and a grinding tribute was imposed. Hezekiah was shut up "like a caged bird within his city," and the walls encircled with siege towers so that none could escape. For a time Hezekiah offered a resistance. Isaiah xxii. 1-14 reflects some of the details of the siege: the armory was put in readiness for attack, the waters collected in the lower pool, and a reservoir made between the two walls for the water of the old pool. The chronicler adds (II. Chron. xxxii.) that all the fountains without the city were closed, and the defences strengthened. Isaiah xxii. 10 also states that certain houses within the city were broken down to fortify the wall. The main army of Sennacherib, however, did not advance against Jerusalem, because it was still occupied in Philistia, or possibly because the scant supply of water furnished by the barren hills of Judah rendered it impracticable.

151. The reason which led Hezekiah to submit, as suggested both by the inscription of Sennacherib and Isaiah xxii. 3, was that the rulers and the allies who had been introduced within the city for its defence were completely terrified by the approach of the foe, "fear overcame them" (Taylor Inscp. iii. 32), and "all fled away together" (Isa. xxii. 3). The same cowardice

evidently characterized the attitude of the leaders at this juncture, as a few days later, when faced by a greater danger. Hezekiah, who was nearly as weak as his craven princes, hastened to send word to Sennacherib, who was then besieging the border town of Lachish: "I have offended; return from me; that which thou puttest upon me will I bear" (II. Kings xviii. 14). He paid for his pardon thirty talents of gold, three hundred talents (eight hundred Assyrian talents according to the inscriptions) of silver, and spoil of every description. To pay this huge tribute, even the gold on the doors of the Temple was stripped off. The daughters of the king and the young men and women of his palace were among the captives who were sent back to Nineveh. Isaiah felt no sympathy with the wild rejoicing which followed this ignominious deliverance, purchased "by the spoiling of the daughter of my people" (Isa. xxii. 1-5). "Let us eat and drink, for to-morrow we shall die" (Isa. xxii. 13) voiced the reckless mood of princes and people.

152. The unnatural mirth of the Jerusalemites was quickly turned to mourning; for the greed of the Assyrian monarch, or else the realization that it would be dangerous to leave such a strong fortress in the hands of those who might become foes as he advanced to the conquest of Egypt, led him to send certain of his officers with a small army to demand the unconditional surrender of the city. Their boasting words struck terror to the hearts of all except one, for it seemed the height of folly to suppose that Jerusalem, weakened as she was, could successfully resist the whole might of the Assyrian army should it be turned against her. In their extremity they turned to Isaiah.

His words of assurance nerved Hezekiah to send back a refusal. The Assyrian messenger found his master at Libnah, having completed the conquest of Lachish. News soon came that the Egyptian king, Tirhakah, was advancing. With the exception of Jerusalem, all Palestine had bowed before Sennacherib, and now he made a last effort to intimidate it into surrender. Of the many crises through which Judah passed, this was the greatest. Surrender meant the destruction of the city and the annihilation of the nation; a refusal to accede to the demands of the conqueror would leave no hope for clemency should the angry king turn his hosts upon them. Again Isaiah came forth to save the city by his inspired and inspiring message: "Assyria's arrogancy and blasphemy shall soon be punished. Jehovah is about to put his hook in its nose and turn it back by the way which it came. The king of Assyria shall not come unto this city, nor shoot an arrow there, neither shall he come before it with shield, nor cast a mount against it" (II. Kings xix. 20-34).

153. Isaiah's greatness is attested, not only by the sublimity of his message, but by the fact that it carried persuasion with it. Sennacherib set out to meet Tirhakah without taking any measures to execute his threats against Jerusalem. On the borders of Egypt he suddenly turned back and never again during his reign visited the west-land. His annals naturally make no reference to this unexpected retreat. The Babylonian chronicle refers to an uprising which may account for his haste. The Egyptian as well as the biblical allusions suggest that, amidst the swampy marshes at the northeastern end of the Nile Delta, his army was attacked by a severe pestilence, which the

Hebrews ever regarded as the work of an angel of Jehovah (compare II. Kings xix. 35 with II. Sam. xxiv. 15, 16), so that he did not dare advance with his forces thus weakened. Whatever was the cause, the fact is established that Isaiah's marvellous prediction was most signally fulfilled, and Judah delivered solely by his activity for another century of remarkable religious development.

VI

THE WORK AND TEACHINGS OF ISAIAH

154. ISAIAH is unquestionably the most perfect example of a Hebrew prophet, for in him every side of the prophetic activity was fully developed. While Micah and Amos were concerned chiefly with social questions, and Hosea with morals and religion, Isaiah spoke with authority on all of these themes. Everything that concerned his nation, and consequently determined its attitude toward Jehovah, whose ambassador he was, commanded his attention. In the politics of his age he was, as we have seen, the central figure. At every turn in the varying fortunes of Judah he proved himself a practical statesman, and a loyal patriot as well. When conditions changed, he urged allegiance to Assyria with as great earnestness as he had formerly opposed the alliance. Unceasingly he combated the social and moral evils of his day, and endeavored to overthrow the popular fallacies by presenting fuller truths. Isaiah's power as a prophet, however, rested more upon the strength of his own personality and his marvellous skill in presenting his teachings, than upon the originality of the truth which he thus made living and vivid; for most of the principles which he emphasized had already been enunciated by Amos and Hosea.

155. Underlying all his teaching was the exalted conception of the holiness of God. It found expression at the time of his call in the words of the seraphim, "Holy, holy, holy is the Lord of hosts; the whole earth is filled with his glory." It was repeated again and again in his prophecies in the designation the "Holy One of Israel," which is his most common title for Jehovah. Already Amos and Hosea had referred to this attribute of the Highest (Amos iv. 2; Hosea xi. 9); and it was a quality commonly ascribed by Semitic peoples to their deities; but Isaiah gave to it a depth of meaning which it had never possessed before. Its original significance appears to have been that of separation. Applied to the gods, it expressed the idea that they were separate from the material world to which their worshippers were confined. Among the Hebrews the conception of physical in time grew into that of moral separation. Jehovah's holiness was his moral perfection as contrasted with man's imperfection. By Isaiah it was used as a comprehensive designation for all of the moral attributes which belong to God. When he declared that Jehovah was the "Holy One of Israel," he meant, on the one hand, that Jehovah stood in an intimate personal relation to his nation. Upon this relationship he based the teaching that God would not allow Jerusalem to be destroyed, and that he would ever preserve at least a remnant of his people. On the other hand, Israel, being in a peculiar sense Jehovah's people, was his representative and under solemn obligation to reflect his character. The social and moral demands which Isaiah constantly urged upon his nation rested upon this unique relationship. "Ye shall be holy, for I am holy"

later expressed the fundamental teaching of priest as well as prophet (Lev. xix. 2; xx. 7, 26).

156. The coming perfection, which he pictured so vividly amidst the darkest scenes of Judah's degradation and disaster, was without doubt primarily intended to serve as a basis of contrast wherewith to bring out the blackness of existing conditions, and at the same time to inspire his countrymen to strive for the speedy realization of that perfection. Although in the highest and truest sense it was an ideal, it was also a prediction and promise of the future, since the inspired prophet was enabled, as his soul's vision was clarified by the Highest, to catch glimpses of the divine plan, and the eternal principles according to which it was gradually unfolding. He saw only the first dawning rays, instead of the sun at its zenith; and consequently he expected in his own generation that which was not realized until centuries later. The details also were often indistinct and determined by the immediate point of view of the prophet; but no one can study his Messianic prophecies and fail to perceive a fundamental rather than a superficial connection between them and the consummation which was inaugurated by Jesus.

157. As he turned from the cowardly Ahaz, whose vacillating policy was plunging his nation into a sea of trouble, his prophetic eyes beheld, instead of the devastation wrought in the north by the armies of Tiglath-Pileser, an era of freedom and peace, to be instituted by a prince yet to be born (ix. 1-7). His character was to be revealed by the names which he would bear: Wonderful Counsellor, with marvellous wisdom directing the policy of his nation; Mighty

God, gifted with divine might and power; Eternal Father, unceasingly caring for his people with paternal solicitude; Prince of Peace, destined to introduce perfect harmony among mankind. Seated upon the throne of David, he was to establish upon the principles of perfect righteousness an eternal kingdom. "The zeal of the Lord of hosts shall perform this." Again, when the armies of Sennacherib had carried destruction to the walls of Jerusalem, Isaiah called attention to this central and personal figure in his picture of the future. "When Jehovah has cut down the proud Assyrians, like the cedars of Lebanon, there shall come forth a shoot out of the stock of Jesse. The spirit of the Lord shall rest upon him, the spirit of wisdom and understanding, the spirit of counsel and might, the spirit of knowledge and of the fear of the Lord." Righteousness shall characterize his rule; the oppressed shall he champion; perfect peace shall prevail, extending even to the animal world, and all the earth shall know the Lord (xi. 1–9).

158. In other prophecies Isaiah presents in varying imagery still other characteristics of the Messianic era. The social abuses, against which he had so often remonstrated, were to cease; men shall be quick to perceive the truth; every act shall receive its just reward; rulers and people alike shall be governed by the laws of justice and mercy (xxxii.). Jerusalem shall be exalted above all the cities of the earth, and thither shall the nations resort to learn the law of Jehovah, the judge of the universe. Isaiah appears to have anticipated that the Messianic kingdom would be an earthly one with its centre at Jerusalem. With Micah (v. 3–6), he seems to have expected that the Messianic

King would appear to inaugurate it during the Assyrian period, and that his first act would be to overthrow the hated conqueror.

159. Isaiah, however, emphasized the moral and spiritual side of the kingdom far more than the temporal. In the prophecy concerning Egypt (xix.), which is generally attributed to him, he declared that in the coming day Egypt and Assyria, which stood for hostile heathendom, would be recognized, on an equality with Israel, as the people of Jehovah. No better illustration could be cited to show the breadth of his vision. To him Jehovah was in a peculiar sense the Holy One of Israel, but he was also the Holy One of the universe, whose just and beneficent purposes were being realized in the rise and fall of nations. Through his eyes one is enabled to follow the unfolding of that divine plan in the varying fortunes which had come and were then coming to his chosen people; and also to trace its outlines, as they were projected on the canvas of the future. Subsequent development was destined to more than fulfil his sublimest predictions, and in a manner far transcending his highest expectations; but posterity has rightly recognized, in the Messianic prophecies of Isaiah and of the prophets who followed him, links binding together the past, the present, and the future, and demonstrating that God's dealings with man are ever prompted by the same loving purpose.

160. The Hebrew prophets recognized that the fulfilment of their predictions rested upon certain conditions, implied if not expressed (compare, for a detailed statement of this important law, Jer. xviii. 3–12). Hence their constant endeavor was to influence their

nation to fulfil the conditions upon which the promises of God were given. Hitherto citizenship in Judah had been regarded as conclusive evidence that a man was a follower of Jehovah, and, consequently, the prophets had spoken to the nation as a whole; but a truer conception of God's character and demands drew sharp distinctions between classes in the Hebrew state itself. Those who accepted and applied the teachings of the true prophets gradually grew into a party having little in common with the majority, who refused to give heed to the new revelation. This little group of disciples corresponded, in the ancient Hebrew commonwealth, to the modern church. It was an inevitable outgrowth of conditions then existing, but it nevertheless marked a new epoch in the history of religion. There is no evidence that the true prophets of the north gained an organized following, and if they did, it was dissipated at the fall of Samaria. Isaiah, however, makes reference to his disciples early in his ministry (viii. 16). To them he turned, when he began to despair of the regeneration of the entire nation. In him the prophetic party found an able leader, and upon them he impressed his teachings. Micah of Moresheth, a younger contemporary of Isaiah, did not share the latter's belief in the inviolability of Zion (Micah iii. 12), but otherwise he echoes in nearly every verse of his prophecy the principles proclaimed by his distinguished teacher. The preservation of so many of the sermons of Isaiah is also doubtless due to the watchful care of his disciples.

161. In this band of faithful hearers and doers the prophet recognized the permanent element in the state, the true Israel, the good grain, which, according to

Amos, was alone to survive the sifting among the nations (ix. 9, 10). They also were the only ones who fulfilled the conditions upon which Jehovah's promises for the future rested; hence Isaiah was led first to give definite expression to the doctrine of the "faithful remnant," which became one of the most important teachings of later prophets.

162. Under Isaiah's leadership the prophetic party was able to exercise a potent influence in Judah. The religious reformation under Hezekiah was one of its fruits. Jeremiah xxvi. 18, 19 associates it definitely with the preaching of Isaiah's disciple, Micah. Unfortunately the references to it are exceedingly general. II. Kings xviii. 4 states that "Hezekiah removed the high places, and brake the pillars, and cut down the Asherah; and he brake in pieces the brazen serpent that Moses had made." Shortly before 701 B. C. Isaiah spoke of the destruction of the idols as a hope of the future (xxx. 22; xxxi. 7), so that the most probable date for these acts is found in the years immediately following the great victory of the prophetic party, in connection with the deliverance of Jerusalem; but it may be questioned whether such a thorough reform as is suggested by the passage in Kings was instituted before the time of Josiah, for in his day he found the high places reared by Solomon near Jerusalem still undisturbed (II. Kings xxiii. 13). The first step would be to destroy the idols of silver and gold and the Asherim, which were so common in the land, and which had called forth the denunciations of Isaiah and Micah. King and people could not be expected to excel in zeal those who instigated the reform, and there is no evidence that these prophets had yet raised their

voices against the high places. Their desecration by the armies of Sennacherib undoubtedly diminished their prestige in contrast with the royal shrine at Jerusalem, which had survived the crisis untouched, and perhaps at this time gave the first impetus to that movement which led later prophets to place them under a ban (Deut. xii.), and ultimately culminated in their abolition by Josiah.

163. The reformation of Hezekiah is not, however, the most lasting fruit of Isaiah's labors. He himself hoped for a national repentance so deep that the people would of their own will cast aside their idols. Not by royal decree, but by word and life, he sought to reform his nation. In his own character he furnished for all time an example of the highest type of patriotism, which shrunk from no sacrifice, nor paled in the face of the greatest danger, because it was inspired by an intelligent and so an unfailing faith in a God of infinite majesty and perfect holiness. Although his field of activity was little Judah, he stands among the greatest statesmen and reformers of the world. He alone saved his nation in the time of its greatest danger. Few, if any, writers have surpassed him in grandeur, force, and vividness of literary style. So forcibly did he impress his teachings by word and by life upon the little group of disciples who gathered about him, that they ultimately transformed the religion of their nation; and since Judaism prepared the way for Christ, Christianity will forever bear the stamp of Isaiah's mighty personality.

VII

THE REACTIONARY REIGN OF MANASSEH

164. WHILE Hezekiah lived, he succeeded in upholding the cause of the prophetical party, to whom he owed the preservation of his kingdom; but when the reins of power were handed over to his youthful son, Manasseh, a great religious reaction swept over Judah. In their zeal, the reform party, instead of patiently waiting until they could reach the heart of the nation, had begun by destroying the popular objects of worship, about which the traditions and veneration of generations had centred. Among all peoples that which is hallowed by sacred associations and endorsed by the past enjoys a peculiar sanctity; but to a remarkable degree was this the case among the primitive Semitic races. In the place of these accepted ideas and sacred relics, the new prophetic school presented a God whom the masses understood only imperfectly, and whose demands were exceedingly difficult for them to fulfil. Isaiah and the author of Micah v. had both given them reason to believe that the Messianic era, which they had pictured in such glowing colors, would be inaugurated immediately after the deliverance of Jerusalem in 701 B. C.; and that with it would come the overthrow of the power of Assyria;

but the monuments show that Judah continued to pay tribute to Assyria for the next half-century, at least, and that, instead of declining, the mighty empire attained its greatest glory during this period. Egypt, toward which it had long been looking with envious eyes, was repeatedly invaded and finally made a subject province. Both the east and the west lay prostrate before the conqueror.

165. The people, who recognized no other index of Jehovah's pleasure or displeasure than prosperity or adversity, considered that they had not only been deluded by the prophetic party, but also led on to commit acts of impiety which were calling down the wrath of their God. Innocent blood was shed in Jerusalem until it was filled from one end to the other (II. Kings xxi. 16). The sword of the reactionists "devoured the prophets like a destroying lion" (Jer. ii. 30). To preach the God of Isaiah became a crime. "Back to the old!" was the popular cry to which Manasseh and the princes who gathered about him listened. The idols torn down by Hezekiah were carefully restored, and the Asherim again set up; the augurs, the enchanters, those who had familiar spirits, and the wizards exercised their old influence (II. Kings xxi. 6). Sodomites were tolerated in connection with the service of the Temple (II. Kings xxiii. 7). In the valley of Hinnom, to the south of Jerusalem, the first born were sacrificed to Moloch (II. Kings xxi. 6; xxiii. 10). Micah vi. 6, 7, reflects the intensity of feeling which prompted such acts. Graphically he puts in the mouth of the people the cry, "Wherewith shall I come before the Lord, and bow myself before the high God? Shall I come before him with burnt offerings, with

calves of a year old? Will the Lord be pleased with thousands of rams, or with ten thousands of rivers of oil? Shall I give my first born for my transgressions, the fruit of my body for the sin of my soul?" As Judah continued to be ground down under the yoke of a foreign conqueror, faith in the old forms was shaken; the masses had not yet accepted the great prophetic truth that Jehovah required his follower simply "to do justly, and to love mercy, and to walk humbly with thy God" (Micah vi. 8); hence they feverishly endeavored to secure the favor of the half-heathenish deity which they worshipped, by the value and multiplicity of their sacrifices.

166. So deep-seated was the popular distrust of Jehovah that the worship of other gods was introduced within his Temple. Naturally those of Assyria received the first place. Already Ahaz had curried favor with his master by imitating Assyrian fashions in the furnishing of the Temple (sect. 134). To those who refused to see with the prophets Jehovah's hand in the conquests of Assyria, as well as in the deliverance of Judah, the humiliation of his chosen people before the world-conqueror was conclusive evidence that his gods were superior to Jehovah. Hence Manasseh strengthened his position with the majority of his subjects, as well as with his Assyrian masters, when "he built altars for all the host of heaven in the two courts of the house of the Lord," and placed the chariots of the sun within the sacred precincts (II. Kings xxi. 3, 4; xxiii. 11, 12). No stronger proof could be adduced to show the inherent weakness of the commonly prevailing conceptions of Jehovah than the readiness with which foreign cults were not only

tolerated but even welcomed. The popular worship of Judah at this time must have been a strange combination of cults, native and foreign. The frantic effort which it made to maintain itself against the attacks of the true prophets and the influence of the new ideas and conditions which confronted it, is only paralleled by the bitter opposition offered by that remarkable mixture of customs and religions which were found in Rome when the light of Christianity first burst upon heathendom.

167. Until the power of Assyria began to wane, the anti-prophetic party remained in control of Judah. The history of this half-century is almost a blank, because the voices of the prophets were silenced. There is evidence, however, that they were not inactive. The spirit and teachings of Isaiah still lived among his disciples. The God who had led his people thus far had not forsaken them. As is always the case, persecution only forced the true prophets to seek other and better channels through which to impart the truths committed to them. Silenced, they took up the pen and endeavored to put their teachings in a form which would be permanent, and at the same time intelligible to all. They recognized that not merely abstract principles, but concrete forms were necessary to reach the masses and take the place of the debasing ceremonials which were valued so highly by the people. Therefore, avoiding the mistakes of Hezekiah's reformation, they adopted, as far as possible, pre-existent usages and traditions, and, eliminating the heathen elements, assigned to them a deeper and more spiritual meaning. The step from the old to the new was thus made easy instead of abrupt.

AIM AND CONTENT OF DEUTERONOMY 163

168. The body of the Book of Deuteronomy (v.-xxvi., xxviii.) is the most important fruit of this new reform movement. Many older laws were incorporated in it, but a majority of the questions with which it deals are those which first became insistent during this period. The reaction under Manasseh had demonstrated that the high places, the local sanctuaries scattered throughout Judah, which up to the time of Hezekiah had been accepted without protest from priest or prophet, were conservers of the practices and forms inherited from the darker past. Their ritual was a snare rather than a help toward the purer worship of Jehovah. Consequently the most prominent enactment of the new law book was to centralize all the ceremonial worship of Jehovah in Jerusalem. The other evils which characterized Manasseh's reign, such as the worship of idols or foreign gods and the consulting of diviners or necromancers, were expressly forbidden. While it is primarily a law book, it is permeated throughout with a broad prophetic spirit. Service is ever placed above sacrifice; to "love and serve Jehovah thy God with all thy heart and all thy soul" (x. 12) is its supreme demand. The love of God toward his people and the love which he asks from them toward him and his creatures are its exalted theme. The detailed laws are presented as a means whereby this love is to find expression. The writer of Deuteronomy was, therefore, like Moses, a prophet, imbued with the great prophetic ideas which were the priceless heritage of his race. Since many of the laws and narratives which are the nucleus of his work were originally Mosaic in spirit, if not in form, their later editor was entirely justified in associating

them, as he does (always in the third person), with the name of Moses. He was only following the custom, characteristic of the compilers of the historical books (compare, for example, I. Sam. viii.) when he reformulated the old laws, and put into the mouth of the father of the Hebrew nation the words which he would have uttered had he lived in the light of the new conditions and fuller revelation.

169. The circumstances of the reign of Manasseh and of his son Amon, who pursued the policy of his father, were unfavorable for the promulgation of this new code; and hence it was laid aside in the Temple until it was discovered — actually or perhaps ostensibly in accordance with a plan known to the few most interested in it — and made the programme of the great reformation of Josiah (II. Kings xxiii.). The Assyrian period of Judean history opened with a religious reform and closed with a reaction which apparently reinstated all the old heathenism; it was filled with grave political errors which brought disaster and bloodshed upon the nation; it was also characterized by awful social and moral crimes; but through all the gloom, God's eternal truth was shining more and more into the hearts of his faithful ones, and through them was finding fuller and clearer expression. The prophetic seed, sown amidst opposition and persecution, was about to take root in the life of the nation.

PART IV

THE BABYLONIAN PERIOD OF JUDAH'S HISTORY

I

THE HISTORICAL SOURCES

170. CERTAIN verses (xxiii. 29-xxiv. 1) in chapters xxii.-xxv. of II. Kings, which treat of the period, were probably based upon material gathered from the state annals; but with the exception of a few later additions, the section as a whole is from the Deuteronomic editor, whose personal knowledge of the events furnished him the necessary data.

171. The Book of Deuteronomy, which, as we have seen (sect. 168), comes from the latter part of the preceding or from the beginning of the Babylonian period, is also a most valuable historical source, since it presents the laws and motives which became the keynotes of the new reformation.

172. The stirring events of the age called forth an unusually large and active body of prophets, many of whose writings have been preserved. The first to raise his voice in denunciation of the sins inherited from Manasseh's reign was Zephaniah. The immediate occasion of his prophecy was the advance of the dreaded Scythians, who about 627 B. C. swept down the eastern coast of the Mediterranean, spreading terror throughout Palestine. From the land of captivity there also came about this time the brief prophecy of

Nahum. Primarily it was intended as a message of encouragement to the Judeans; but its theme is the coming fall of the cruel, rapacious world-conqueror, Assyria, whose yoke had rested upon the necks of the Semitic peoples for more than two centuries. It was probably evoked by the first attack upon Nineveh, in 625 B. C., by the Medes under King Phraortes. To the same group belongs the powerful prophecy of Habakkuk. Josiah's brilliant reign has been succeeded by the reactionary rule of Jehoiakim. The Assyrians have completely disappeared, and in their place the Chaldeans are advancing. The date of the prophecy, therefore, must be sought shortly before the great battle of Carchemish in 604 B. C.

173. The chief historical source for the entire period is the combination of prophecy, history, and biography found in the Book of Jeremiah. The first collection of his discourses was made in the fourth year of Jehoiakim (xxxvi.), but was soon destroyed. The second edition, which was made in the following year and included his earlier sermons, is probably the basis of our present text. Jeremiah's ministry, however, began twenty-three years earlier, in 627 B. C., before the reformation of Josiah had been instituted, and lasted until after the final destruction of Jerusalem in 586 B. C. His sermons in their present order are not arranged chronologically. Fortunately the superscriptions, as well as the contents, aid in determining the dates at which they were delivered. His call, recorded in chapter i., belongs to the year 627 B. C. The sermons in ii.-vi. refer frequently to "the foe from the north," which was probably the Scythian hordes alluded to by Zephaniah, although when he collected

his prophecies later he had the Chaldeans in mind. They were, therefore, originally delivered soon after the prophet's call in 627 B. C., and represent his noble contributions to the reformation, which was carried into effect in 621 B. C. Chapter xi. 1-8 suggests the important part which he took in that movement. The short section, xxii. 10-12, relates to the brief reign of Jehoahaz.

174. Jeremiah's activity at the beginning of the reign of Jehoiakim is represented by chapters xxvi., vii.-ix., x. 17-25, xi. 9-xii. 6. To the year 604 B. C. may be assigned the sermons and incidents recorded in chapters xxv., xxxvi. 1-8, xlv. 1-xlix. 33. Chapter xxxvi. 9-32 belongs to the following year, and xiv.-xx. and xxxv. to the latter part of the reign of Jehoiakim. About the death of that inefficient ruler and the first siege of Jerusalem in 597 B. C. are grouped xii. 7-xiii. 27 and xxii. 13-30. Chapters xxiv., xxvii.-xxix., and xlix. 34-39 come from the earlier days of Zedekiah's reign; while l. and li. contain a prophecy which, according to li. 59, belongs to the year 593 B. C., but its point of view, style, and temper are so different from those which characterize Jeremiah's ordinary utterances that it is usually assigned to one of his disciples who wrote not long before the end of the Babylonian exile. The siege of Jerusalem by Nebuchadrezzar, which began in 587 B. C., called forth the series of sermons preserved in xxi. 1-10, xxiii., and xxxiv. Chapters xxxvii. and xxxviii. are historical, and describe the personal experiences of the prophet during the siege. The glorious prophecies contained in xxx.-xxxiii. are from the same dark period; the last two are definitely assigned

to the days of his confinement during the second stage of the siege. Chapters xxxix.–xliv. and lii. record the final capture of Jerusalem and the subsequent fortunes of Jeremiah and the few who were allowed by the conqueror to remain in Judah. Respecting the second edition of Jeremiah's earlier sermons, it is explicitly stated that "there were added besides unto them many like words" (xxxvi. 32). The example set by the prophet himself was followed by later editors of his writings, who recast certain sections and inserted others. The historical chapters, also, are either from Baruch, his faithful scribe, or from some one of his disciples.

175. Among the prominent Jewish exiles who were transported in 597 B. C. to the banks of the river Chebar in Babylonia, was a priest by the name of Ezekiel. In July of 592 B. C., the fifth year of his captivity, he was called by a vision to the prophetic office. The chief end of his life-work was to conserve within the little body of exiles that which was best in the religious heritage from his nation's past; but while Jerusalem still stood, conditions there frequently commanded his attention. Consequently the first twenty-four chapters of his prophecy contain much valuable historical data relating to Judah. With characteristic exactness he has dated all of his prophecies. Chapters i.–vii. come from the year 592, viii.–xix. from 591, xx.–xxiii. from 590, and xxiv. from 588 B. C. The foreign prophecies (xxv.–xxxii.), like Obadiah's brief oracle against Edom, suggest the attitude of the surrounding nations at the time of Jerusalem's final fall. While Ezekiel's writings lack the intimate familiarity with the details of Judah's later history which

characterizes those of Jeremiah, they contain the conclusions of a man gifted with clearest insight into conditions and forces within and without the parent state.

176. It is fortunate that the biblical records for the period are so full and varied, for the outside sources throw little light upon the history of Judah. The inscriptions of Nebuchadrezzar, thus far discovered, relate almost entirely to his building enterprises and devotion to the gods. Nothing respecting his invasion and capture of Jerusalem has been found. With the aid of Herodotus and Babylonian records it is possible, however, to trace the outlines of the history of the great eastern nations which determined the fate of the little Palestinian kingdom.

II

THE GREAT REFORMATION UNDER JOSIAH

177. AMON, the son of Manasseh, was slain by his nobles after a reign of only two years. The people thereupon arose and put the conspirators to death. Unfortunately the author of Kings leaves us to conjecture the motives which prompted these acts. He only states that Amon "walked in all the way his father walked in, and served the idols that his father served" (II. Kings xxi. 21). His policy was calculated to win the favor of the masses, who clung tenaciously to their old idols; hence their zeal in avenging his death is explained. Whether or not the conspiracy of the nobles represented a premature attempt to institute a more progressive religious policy, must remain an open question, although subsequent developments strengthen the inference that it was. If so, it indicates that already, when Josiah, the little eight-year-old son of Amon, came to the throne of Judah in 639 B. C., the spirit of reform was in the air. Conditions were also favorable. Already omens of Assyria's coming downfall were beginning to appear. The predictions of Isaiah were at last about to be fulfilled. Assyrian armies no longer menaced the peace of Palestine. The gods of the conqueror were seen, after all, to be not invincible. The work of the reformers also began to be felt. The ardor with which the descendant of such immediate ancestors as Amon and Manasseh later championed the cause of Jehovah is explained only on the supposition that Josiah at an early age came under the instruction of these earnest co-workers.

178. Of necessity, they developed their plans at first in secret, awaiting a favorable occasion to raise openly the standard of reform. This came about the twelfth year of Josiah's reign, when the startling news spread throughout Palestine that a detachment of the Scythians was moving southward along the coast of the Mediterranean. A more dreaded foe could not be imagined. From their home north of the Black Sea, they streamed through the passes of the Caucasus in countless hordes, ruthlessly destroying cities, fields, men, women, and children. They knew neither fear nor mercy. Already strong nations had fallen before them, and even the Assyrian empire was shaken to its foundations; therefore the Judeans had good reason to tremble at the approach of the mysterious foe. From Herodotus we learn that they advanced to the borders of Egypt, where they were bribed by the reigning Pharaoh to turn back. The coast towns of Palestine bore the brunt of their attack. Although there is no evidence that they invaded Judah, their presence shook its inhabitants from their indifference.

179. Zephaniah seized the opportunity to attack the sins of his nation. Religious conditions were practically the same as under Manasseh, except that the bitterness which characterized the first stages of the

reaction had disappeared, and the prophets of Jehovah could speak freely, without fear of persecution. Within the capital the black-robed priests of Baal were still supported by eager devotees. On the house-tops many continued to worship the sun, moon, and stars. Some dragged Jehovah down to a level with the heathen deities by syncretizing him with Malcam; while others had completely abandoned his service (i. 4-6). Among the nominal worshippers of Jehovah there were many who had arrived at the sceptical conclusion that he lacked either the desire or the power to direct the affairs of man (i. 12). To all the prophet declared that the great oncoming host was God's instrument of judgment. Forcibly he portrayed the utter desolation which was about to come upon proud Assyria, and upon the circle of hostile nations which had taken base advantage of Judah's weakness (ii.); but declared, as Amos had on another occasion (sect. 81), that the destruction would not stop there. "Against the inhabitants of Jerusalem, Jehovah will stretch out his hand and cut off the apostates (i. 4, 5), and the princes who are as roaring lions, the judges who are as evening wolves, the light and treacherous prophets and the priests who profane the sanctuary and do violence to the law" (iii. 3, 4). The proclamation of judgment, however, was always with the prophets only a means to an end. With the same beauty and grandeur Zephaniah proceeds to describe the other side of the coming day of Jehovah. When the nation has been purged of its dross, then Jehovah will gather the "meek of the earth, who have wrought judgment" (ii. 3), "the remnant of Israel," and "they shall feed and lie down, and none shall make them afraid," and he "will make them a name and a praise among all the peoples of the earth" (iii. 13, 20). To his countrymen this little reform tract was a signal of warning before the coming storm, and at the same time it pointed the way to a haven of refuge for the faithful.

180. At this critical period (627 B. C.) the voice of the Lord calling him to be a prophet was first recognized by Jeremiah. His book of prophecies, which in many parts is almost a personal memoir, tells of the conflicts which then raged in the heart of the timid youth. He appreciated in part the magnitude of the task to which he was called (i. 11-19). Although he loved his nation passionately, he was destined to witness the hideous death-struggles which were induced by its excesses. Rejected and persecuted by those whom he sought to help, his life was to be one prolonged martyrdom, doubly painful because he was so keenly sensitive. In character and experience he had much in common with Hosea. Among all the prophets, none uttered sterner denunciations and none spoke with greater tenderness. In the spirituality and the depth of his religious emotions he had no equal. Jeremiah's birthplace was the little town of Anathoth, situated a short distance north of Jerusalem. Thither Abiathar, the priestly representative of the house of Eli, had been banished by Solomon (I. sect. 141); and it is by no means impossible that the prophet was a descendant of that renowned family. In his birth and in the holy influences cast about him by his parents during his childhood, he recognized an especial preparation for the prophetic office (i. 5).

181. "Out of the north evil shall break forth upon

all the inhabitants of the land" (i. 14), was a thought prominent at the time of his call and, as with Zephaniah, was the background of his reformation sermons. He was not obliged to look far for the cause of this evidence of Jehovah's displeasure. The hideous fruits of Judah's apostasy were apparent on every side; it was almost impossible to find a just and true man in Jerusalem (v. 1). The prophet felt that awful loneliness which oppressed him throughout most of his ministry. "If thou wilt put away thine abominations out of my sight, then shalt thou not be removed" (iv. 1), was the central idea of his preaching during these years.

182. Zephaniah and Jeremiah did not stand alone in their noble endeavor to reform the nation. Nahum's brief prophecy came about this time, to assure the Judeans that Jehovah was about to cast down the haughty Assyrians. Common adversity led the more faithful priests and prophets to draw closely together. The high-priest Hilkiah, the friend of Jeremiah, was prominent in the movement; and certain of Josiah's ministers, as well as the king himself, were most favorably disposed toward it. The first open steps toward reform seem to have been taken about 627 B.C., when Zephaniah and Jeremiah began to preach. Already the Temple was being repaired, when, in 621 B.C., the memorable discovery was made which determined the character of the reformation. The custom, initiated in the days of Joash (sect. 119), of intrusting the funds for the repair of the Temple to a committee, consisting of the royal scribe or secretary and the chief priest, was still in vogue. While they were discharging this duty, Hilkiah, the priest, in-

formed Shaphan, the scribe, of the discovery of the book of the law within the Temple. It was given to Shaphan, who read it and then delivered it to the king. When the king had heard its contents, he was deeply affected. Forthwith he despatched a deputation, consisting of Hilkiah, the priest, Achbor, Asaiah, Shaphan and his son, Ahikam, to inquire of the Lord, in behalf of himself and the people, respecting the significance of the book. Strangely enough, they turned, not to Zephaniah or Jeremiah, but to Huldah, a prophetess, the wife of the keeper of the wardrobe. When its contents were confirmed by the prophetess, the king gathered together all the people of his realm within the Temple precincts and read the book to them. As a result, a solemn covenant was entered into by king and people to observe its injunctions.

183. Rigorous measures were at once instituted by the king to carry those injunctions into effect. The first step was to cleanse the Temple. The vessels and paraphernalia which were used in the service of Baal and the host of heaven were brought forth and burned in the Kidron valley; the altars reared by Manasseh were demolished; the chariots of the sun were burned, and their horses removed from the entrance of the Temple; the houses of those consecrated to the licentious worship of Baal and Ashtarte were torn down; in the valley of Hinnom, Tophet, where the people had been wont to sacrifice their children to Molech, was defiled; the shrines erected by Solomon without the city, for Ashtoreth, Chemosh, and other foreign divinities, were broken in pieces. The king's zeal even led him to destroy the old Israelitish sanctuary of Bethel. Idols and teraphim were placed under a ban, and

wizards and diviners driven from the land. The most revolutionary act, however, was the destruction of the high places, which were found near every city. The kings of Judah, in recognition of the importance of those places, had heretofore appointed regular priests to care for them. Deprived of their occupation, these were invited by Josiah to connect themselves with the Temple at Jerusalem, which was made by this religious revolution the one legal sanctuary in the kingdom. As might be expected, the majority of them rejected the offer, and "did eat unleavened bread among their brethren" (II. Kings xxiii. 9). In conclusion a memorable passover feast was celebrated at Jerusalem in accordance with the directions laid down in the newly found law book.

184. Conclusive evidence might be adduced from other sources to demonstrate that this book of the covenant consisted of a portion, at least, of our present Book of Deuteronomy; but it is sufficient to note how closely the reformation instituted by Josiah conforms in every detail to the laws therein contained. Heretofore we have found that custom and usage, frequently radically different from those which are enjoined by the first five books of the Old Testament, determined the character of the ceremonial forms in force at any given period; but with the reformation of Josiah begins the rule of the written law. At first this undoubtedly represented a great advance, for not only were the requirements of Deuteronomy far superior to the forms which they supplanted, but they also gave a stability to the worship of Jehovah which it had never possessed before. Reactions came, but the written law survived to gain wider acceptance when conditions

were again favorable. Ultimately, however, the means whereby this stability had been secured impeded the religious development of the Jewish race, as is always the case when fixed forms of worship or statements of faith are substituted for the living spiritual life which they were intended to promote. The law was allowed to overshadow and extinguish prophecy, from which it originally derived its spiritual significance; and when it ceased to grow, it became dead and meaningless.

185. The Book of Deuteronomy was, as we have seen (sect. 168), the result of a noble effort to replace the popular religion with a new system in accord with the new prophetic revelation. The most practical way of reaching the masses seemed to be through explicit laws, which would regulate social relations and the religious cult. Deuteronomy, accordingly, sought to give objective expression to the fundamental prophetic teachings. The abolition of idols and of the worship of foreign deities was the most impressive declaration that Jehovah was a spirit, and that he, as the supreme ruler of the universe, demanded the entire homage of his followers. The great prophetic watchword, "Thou art a holy people unto the Lord thy God," which finds expression so frequently in Deuteronomy (vii. 6; xiv. 2, 21; xxvi. 1, 9; xxviii. 9), was interpreted into the details of life and ritual. Isaiah's other characteristic doctrine of the inviolability of Zion also took form in the exaltation of the Temple at Jerusalem, to the exclusion of all other sanctuaries.

186. The full significance of this sweeping innovation can be appreciated only by a comparison with the practices which it supplanted. Hitherto sacrifices appear to have been offered anywhere and by any one;

in fact, every animal slain was regarded as shared with the deity (I. sects. 69, 70). At every town there was a high place to which the people went, not only on feast days, but whenever they wished, through the priest, to have a disputed case settled, or to ascertain the divine will respecting their private matters (I. sect. 163). Religion entered into all their life. The enactments of Deuteronomy swept away the high places, placed a ban upon private sacrifice, and restricted all offerings to the Temple. A sharp distinction was thereby drawn between the laity and the priests, between secular and holy things. Religion henceforth became something formal, above and apart, rather than in all which concerned the nation or individual. Conventionality took the place of the old freedom and joyousness which had so often degenerated into laxness. The end desired by the reformers was attained. The narrowing of religion saved it from the shallowness of heathenism. The Jehovah who was worshipped in the Temple with jealously guarded forms was not in danger of being degraded to a level with the surrounding deities. That which henceforth constituted the Jewish church was divorced from the state, and so survived the downfall of the nation. Unfortunately the narrowing process did not cease after the crisis was past, so that its later effects were deplorable; but, measured in the light of existing circumstances, the reformation of Josiah marks the beginning of that movement which ultimately resulted in the complete elimination of the practical heathenism which had long threatened the extinction of the pure worship of Jehovah.

187. The unparalleled success of the reformation of

Josiah was undoubtedly largely due to the ability and energy of the king himself. Since David, no ruler appeared on the throne of Judah who has been so universally commended by his own and succeeding generations. His reformation, like every other instituted by state authority, affected first the externals of religion; but the thirteen prosperous years which followed were improved to impress its fundamental principles upon the popular heart. In Jeremiah xi. 1-8, we may listen to the exhortations of the prophet as he went about the cities of Judah and the streets of Jerusalem preaching in the language of Deuteronomy, "Hear ye the words of this covenant, and do them." Prophet, priest, and wise man united with voice and pen in heralding the glorious truths which then for the first time received general acceptance. The prophetical party carried all before it, and heathenism was for the time driven into concealment. The Messianic era foretold by earlier prophets seemed about to become a reality. The principles of justice and mercy dominated rulers and people (Jer. xxii. 15, 16). Peace and prosperity bespoke Jehovah's favor.

188. The reformation of Josiah furnishes the best starting-point from which to study the literature of the Old Testament. It kindled a prodigious literary activity, and has left its impress upon nearly every volume of that unique library. The language, ideas, and spirit which find expression in Deuteronomy and Jeremiah characterize all the writings of the age, making it possible readily to distinguish them. It now becomes easy to understand the work of the first editors of the prophetico-historical books, Judges, Samuel, and Kings, who gathered together the ancient

narratives of their race, calling attention to the rich spiritual truths which they illustrated, and interspersing them with observations and judgments which reflect the higher ideals current at this later period. Some of the Psalms bear witness to the deeply devotional spirit which then filled the souls of these earnest workers. The introduction to the Book of Proverbs (i.–ix.), whose hortatory religious tone stands in such contrast with the other sections of the anthology, contains the characteristic birth-marks of this unique epoch. The union of the older collections found in chapters x.–xxix. of Proverbs is probably the work of the same hand. The priceless revelation granted to the Hebrew race had begun to crystallize into written proverbs, psalms, prophecies, and laws, so that when reactions and exile came, it was preserved to be the imperishable and inestimable heritage of humanity.

III

JUDAH AND THE NEW WORLD POWERS

189. JUDAH'S Indian summer ended most abruptly. The primary cause of this time of peace and prosperity had been the decline of Assyria. Two decades before its final disintegration, Nahum beheld in prophetic vision a fierce enemy marching against this "den of lions" which was filled with the prey of nations, and, in the name of Jehovah, pronounced a woe upon it. He saw that its "people were women, and the gates of its land were set wide open unto its enemies." Disorganization and social corruption had sapped its strength; "its hurt was grievous." Already the prophet heard the nations clapping their hands over the downfall of their merciless oppressor. The first serious attack came from the Medes, about the middle of the seventh century. Hostilities were temporarily interrupted by the invasion of the Scythians; but when these ceased, the Medes, under Cyaxares, united with the Babylonians, under Nabopolassar, for the final overthrow of the mighty power whose name for more than two centuries had been written in blood on almost every page of Semitic history; and its former vassals, the Babylonians (or Chaldeans, as they are more commonly called), succeeded to its rule.

190. Before Nineveh fell in 607 B. C., Necho, the aspiring Pharaoh of Egypt, set out to secure a portion of the great empire which was falling into decay. The march of his huge army lay across the memorable plain of Esdraelon. Josiah, who had improved the period of quiet to extend the boundaries of Judah so that they enclosed a large part of the territory of ancient Israel, refused Necho a passage across Hebrew soil. Blindly casting himself upon the care of Jehovah, whose cause he had so valiantly championed, the reformer-king with his little army attacked the Egyptian host, doubtless confident that his God would grant him the victory. At the old fortress of Megiddo he fell slain, and the conqueror passed on, assured of Judah's submission.

191. The death of Josiah is unquestionably the most tragic event in Hebrew history, for his fall proved a death-blow to the immediate realization of the ideals of the party which he represented. The reformation instituted under his direction was still on trial. The heathen party, who had only been forced into silence, hastened to point to the signal calamity which befell him as a judgment upon his iconoclastic zeal. The force of this line of argument with the people had already been frequently demonstrated. Since Necho did not immediately follow up his victory at Megiddo, the prophetical party was able to set aside Josiah's eldest son, whose disregard for their interest was known, and place his brother, Jehoahaz, on the throne. The new king, however, did not have an opportunity to vindicate the confidence which was placed in him. When the Egyptian conqueror returned from the Euphrates, whither he had extended his rule, he en-

THE RULE OF JEHOIAKIM

ticed Jehoahaz to Riblah, on the river Orontes, where he was holding court. For some reason — perhaps because the Judean king represented the party of Josiah, or because his older brother promised greater tribute — Necho sent Jehoahaz, after a reign of only three months, in chains to Egypt, and made his brother Eliakim, who bore after his accession the name of Jehoiakim, king in his stead.

192. This act placed the reactionary, half-heathenish party in control of the state, and inaugurated the series of political errors and religious crimes which resulted, in less than a quarter of a century, in the complete destruction of Judah. The tribute imposed by Necho was comparatively small, consisting of one hundred talents of silver and one of gold; but it was exacted from the people, while the king devoted the wealth which must have collected in the public treasury during Josiah's prosperous reign, together with that which he unjustly extorted from his subjects, to building for himself a broad and spacious palace, provided with windows, ceiled with cedar, and painted with vermilion (Jer. xxii. 13-15). The chief ambition of this selfish, vain son of a noble father was to imitate the luxurious courts on the Nile and Euphrates. Solomon's policy of despotism was re-introduced into little Judah, and with it came its inevitable fruits, oppression and injustice (Jer. xxii. 17). Judah's "shepherds had become brutish and ceased to inquire of the Lord" (Jer. x. 21). The rigorous demands of the true prophets were treated with contempt. The majority of the Judeans followed the example of their king, and "turned back to the iniquities of their forefathers and went after other gods to serve them"

(Jer. xi. 10). Most of the heathen practices of Manasseh's reign were resumed. "Their children remembered their altars and their Asherim by the green trees upon the high hills" (Jer. xvii. 2). Altars to Baal were set up in all the cities of Judah and in every street of Jerusalem (Jer. xi. 13). In attempting to root out the old cult at one stroke and by force, the reformers had essayed a task which has repeatedly been proved impossible.

193. While the ignorant were turning back to their old idols and heathen gods, the more enlightened were entertaining a fatal delusion. Shutting their eyes to the dangers which threatened their nation from without, they blindly trusted to the service of the Temple to save them (Jer. vii. 4). Isaiah's teaching respecting the inviolability of Zion had grown into a dogma, and the conditions upon which that teaching had been based were ignored. Formalism, instead of morality, was regarded as the essential element in religion. In vain Jeremiah endeavored to recall them to their senses: "Will you steal, murder, commit adultery, swear falsely, burn incense unto Baal, and walk after other gods whom you have not known, and then come and stand before me in this house which is called by my name, and say, We are delivered; that you may do all these abominations? This Temple has become a den of robbers. It shall be utterly destroyed, as was the ancient sanctuary at Shiloh (I. sect. 60). You shall be cast out as were your brethren of the north. On just one condition can this nation be saved, and that is that it amend its way" (vii. 3–15).

194. During this period Jeremiah stood almost alone. He complains that the people put their trust

in lying words that cannot profit; priest and prophet deal falsely; in their pride they declare, We are wise and the law of the Lord is with us; constantly they are crying, Peace, peace, when there is no peace (vii. 8; viii. 8, 11). His own kinsmen at Anathoth treacherously attempted to put him to death because he would not stop uttering his ominous predictions (xi. 18–23). So deep-seated was the popular faith in the indestructibility of Jerusalem that his opponents, the priests and prophets, preferred a capital charge against him because he had prophesied against the city (xxvi.). It was a critical moment for the prophet. Calmly he reiterated his former words, and warned his accusers against bringing innocent blood upon their capital. His voice might then have been silenced, had not certain of the elders, chief among whom was Ahikam, the son of Josiah's secretary, Shaphan, saved him by citing the precedent of Micah, the Morashtite, who had declared in the days of Hezekiah, "Zion shall be ploughed as a field, and Jerusalem shall become heaps, and the mountain of the house as the high places of a forest" (Micah iii. 12). Uriah, a prophet of the town of Kiriath-jearim, who prophesied, as did Jeremiah, respecting the fate of the city and land, had no powerful patrons to espouse his cause. Persecution by the king and princes led him to flee to Egypt, whither Jehoiakim sent messengers, who brought him back and then slew him, casting his body into the common burial field. The murder of this early martyr indicates the temper of king and people, which led the few true prophets, like Jeremiah, to realize that the fate of the nation was sealed.

195. The rule of Egypt over Palestine lasted only

four years. After the capture of Nineveh the Chaldeans soon conquered the territory of the fallen foe; and in 605-604 B. C. Nebuchadrezzar (wrongly written Nebuchadnezzar in the Books of Kings and Chronicles), the son of Nabopolassar, met Necho in a memorable battle near the town of Carchemish, on the Euphrates. Jeremiah xlvi. re-echoes the din of that fierce conflict: Egypt's "mighty ones were beaten down, they fled away and looked not back; their swift and mighty men stumbled and fell." The advance of the conqueror was delayed by the death of his father. Two or three years elapsed before he could establish himself upon the throne, and again turn westward to reap the fruits of the victory which left him master of southwestern Asia.

196. **The impending advance of the Chaldeans** gave new force to the warnings of the true prophets. Before his armies reached Judah Jeremiah proclaimed with the most absolute assurance that Nebuchadrezzar would lay Judah desolate, and that the nations about would also be compelled to drink of this winecup of fury from the hand of Jehovah (xxv.). Habakkuk voices the cry of doubt and anguish which escaped at this time from the lips of the few faithful followers of Jehovah: "Within Judah the law is relaxed, justice perverted, violence rules, while the fierce and pitiless Chaldeans are sweeping down upon us for our destruction. Thou that art of purer eyes than to behold evil, and that canst not look on perverseness, wherefore lookest thou on them that deal treacherously, and holdest thy peace when the wicked swallows up the man that is more righteous than he?" With Jeremiah, he realized that the overweening pride of their foes would ulti-

mately prove their destruction (Jer. xxv. 12; Hab. ii. 8); but for the present there was nothing for the just man to do but wait and trust that his integrity would yet be vindicated (ii. 4). These words of warning may have been that which influenced the Judeans to submit without resistance when Nebuchadrezzar advanced, about 600 B. C., to the conquest of the westland. After three years, however, they entered upon that mad career of revolt which darkens the last chapters of Judah's history.

IV

JEREMIAH AND THE FALL OF JERUSALEM

197. VIEWED in the perspective of history, the most important character in this closing period of Hebrew history is Judah's last and greatest prophet. Throughout the reign of Jehoiakim, however, Jeremiah's words were treated only with contempt. At times discouraged, but never daunted, he constantly sought new means whereby to make an impression upon his unwilling hearers. When the approach of the Chaldeans, after the battle of Carchemish, had led to the proclamation of a national fast at Jerusalem, he seized the opportunity to collect his former prophecies, and then himself despatched his faithful scribe, Baruch, to the Temple to read them in the presence of the people (xxxvi.). A grandson of Josiah's secretary, Shaphan, hastened to inform the princes assembled in the palace; and Baruch was forthwith summoned to read his roll before them. As they listened they were so far impressed by its contents that they determined to bring it to the attention of the king. Knowing his dislike for the uncompromising prophecies of Jeremiah, they kindly urged Baruch to flee with his master into concealment. Then they informed Jehoiakim of the affair, and at his command the roll was brought. Before many pages had been read, he contemptuously cut it into pieces, and cast it into a fire that was burning on a brazier such as those with which the Hebrews heated their homes during the cold winter months. The remonstrances of certain of his ministers, who were friendly to Jeremiah, were in vain. Three of the nobles were at once sent out to take the prophet and his faithful scribe; "but the Lord hid them."

198. Two or three years later, when the spirit of revolt was sweeping Judah into fatal opposition to Babylon, Jeremiah redoubled his efforts to bring the infatuated people to their senses. The political policy which he advocated was the same as that urged by Isaiah under strikingly similar circumstances. To the party who were relying upon Egypt to save them from Babylon, he said, "Cursed is he that trusteth in man, and maketh flesh his arm. God alone is the true source of confidence; for as the clay in the potter's hand, so are you, O house of Israel, in the hand of Jehovah; therefore, amend your ways if you desire deliverance" (xvii. 5, 7; xviii. 6, 11). There was, however, no hope, for the people were bent upon following their own devices (xviii. 12).

199. In 597 B. C. Jehoiakim openly revolted. The other states of Palestine, instead of joining with him, overran the territory of Judah at the instigation of their Babylonian master. Among those who then sought refuge in Jerusalem were men of the tribe of the Recabites, descendants of the wandering Kenites, who had tenaciously clung to their nomadic life and customs. Knowing the steadfastness with which they adhered to the strict injunctions of their great reformer, Jonadab (II. Kings x. 15-24), Jeremiah invited

them into the Temple and placed wine before them. As he had anticipated, they bluntly refused to partake. Thereupon he turned to the Judeans and drew a forcible contrast between their disregard for the commands of Jehovah, as proclaimed by his prophets, and the fidelity of the Recabites in following the precepts of their ancestor. At another time Jeremiah led certain of the elders of Jerusalem out into the valley of Hinnom, which had often been defiled by human sacrifices, and solemnly broke before them a potter's vessel, which he had brought with him (xix.). Then he declared in the name of Jehovah: "Even so will I break this people and city." When he repeated his prophecy in the court of the Temple, he was violently attacked and put in the public stocks by Pashur, the chief officer of the house of the Lord (xx.). When the crowds, as they passed by, derided him, his humanity asserted itself; bitterly he cursed the day of his birth, and prayed that he might see Jehovah's vengeance upon his persecutors (xx. 12); but, painful as was his lot, he still went on prophesying, for, as he pathetically exclaims: "If I say I will not speak any more in his name, then there is in mine heart as it were a burning fire shut up in my bones, and I am weary with forbearing, so that I cannot stay (xx. 9).

200. Death removed Jehoiakim before he saw the final results of his folly in revolting against Babylon. He was succeeded by his eighteen-year-old son, Coniah, or Jeconiah (Jer. xxii. 24; xxiv. 1), who assumed at his accession the name Jehoiakin. The queen mother, Nehushta, appears to have been the virtual ruler (Jer. xxii. 26). It was, however, a barren reign, lasting only three months. The circle of Judah's enemies was

ever drawing closer and closer. The cities outside Jerusalem were abandoned to their fate (Jer. xiii. 19). In vain the Judeans looked toward Egypt for help, for Nebuchadrezzar had barred his rival out of Palestine (II. Kings xxiv. 7). At last a division of the army of the great conqueror was detailed to lay siege to the capital, and the pride of the king and queen-mother was humbled (Jer. xiii. 18). Seeing that resistance was hopeless, they with their court surrendered unconditionally on the arrival of the Babylonian monarch. In their treatment of rebellious states the Chaldeans followed the policy of the Assyrians. Jehoiakin was carried away to Babylon. During the latter part of his exile he was kindly treated by his captors (Jer. lii. 31-34), and was regarded with marked respect by his subjects, who shared his captivity (Ezek. i. 2; Lam. iv. 20). With him went the best elements in Judah. In addition to the nobles and court, Nebuchadrezzar carried off seven thousand trained warriors and one thousand artisans. In many cases, although not always (Ezek. xxiv. 21), their families went with them to swell the numbers in the Jewish colony, which was established on the river Chebar in the land of the Chaldeans (Ezek. i. 3). To pay the heavy tribute exacted by the conqueror, palace and Temple were looted. Bitterly did those who were left behind feel the loss of the vessels of the Lord's house, which went to furnish Babylonian temples (Jer. xxvii. 16; Dan. i. 2; v. 2). Only the pillars, the brazen sea, the vases, and the less valuable vessels were left behind (Jer. xxvii. 18).

201. Those who were carried into exile at the first captivity, in 597 B. C., had proved themselves base

enough; but even Jeremiah called them good in comparison with the ignorant, inefficient men who were allowed to remain. Over these Nebuchadrezzar placed, as his vassal, Mattaniah, a younger son of Josiah, who is known in history by his official name, Zedekiah. The situation called for a ruler who could organize and then hold these turbulent elements to a wise and consistent policy. Under the Assyrian rule, Judah had bent before the storm and thus survived; the Chaldeans were no harsher taskmasters. Unfortunately, however, the new king was lacking in both energy and courage. Although his intentions were good, he proved only a tool in the hands of his headstrong nobles.

202. The overwhelming disaster, which had come upon Judah, instead of leading the people to listen to the voice of the true prophets, only prompted them to cry more vehemently: "The Lord seeth us not; the Lord hath forsaken the land" (Ezek. viii. 12; ix. 9). Having lost faith in Jehovah, they turned to the old superstitions. The ancient totemistic forms of worship were secretly revived in connection with the Temple; an Asherah was again set up within the sacred precincts: the women adopted the Syrian custom of weeping for Tammuz; and the men worshipped the sun, turning their backs upon Jehovah's sanctuary (Ezek. viii.). The siren voices of the false prophets, who deliberately or mistakenly uttered lying messages in the name of Jehovah, continued to lure the nation on to its ruin.

203. Soon after the accession of Zedekiah, messengers came from the vassal kings of Moab, Ammon, and Tyre, urging him to join in a league against

Babylon. Chapters xxvii. and xxviii. of Jeremiah's prophecy reflect the bitter conflict which was then waged between him and those "who prophesied lies." The methods and form of expression used by each were identical, so that it is not strange that the people found it difficult to decide which to believe. Jeremiah's advice was: "Serve the king of Babylon, and live." His opponents, chief among whom was the prophet Hananiah, declared that Jehovah had broken the yoke of Babylon, and that within two years Jehoiakin, with the captives and spoil taken by Nebuchadrezzar, would be brought back to Jerusalem. To impress his words, Hananiah took the yoke which Jeremiah was wearing about his neck, as a symbol of the continued rule of Babylon, and broke it in pieces before the people, saying, "Even so will Jehovah break the yoke of Nebuchadrezzar within two full years from off the neck of all the nations." For the moment Jeremiah was silenced; but he soon returned with the message that the broken yoke of wood was to be exchanged for a yoke of iron, and that within a year Hananiah would atone for his lying words with his life. The death of this degenerate prophet undoubtedly did more than anything else to establish in the minds of the people the truth of Jeremiah's predictions and save their state temporarily from fatal entanglements.

204. The fanatical belief, however, that Jehovah would interpose in a miraculous way to rescue his people from the hands of their enemies was also shared by many of the exiles. False prophets and prophetesses in their midst encouraged them in the delusion, so that Ezekiel, like Jeremiah, with whom he was in perfect agreement, recognized that his influence was

constantly being neutralized. Popular faith in the prophetic word was practically destroyed, and with it that veneration which had heretofore guarded the person of the ambassador of the Highest. Communication between the exiles and their brethren in Judah was frequent; and despite the efforts of Jeremiah and Ezekiel, the two kindled each other's fanatical hopes until, in 588 B. C., those in Judah plunged into another revolt against Babylon. Ammon and Tyre joined with them, and ambassadors were despatched to Egypt to secure "horses and much people" (Ezek. xvii. 15). Nebuchadrezzar gave the rebellion his immediate attention, and by January of 587 B. C. was encamped with his army about the walls of Jerusalem. In their terror and dismay its inhabitants were induced to observe the neglected law, incorporated in Deuteronomy xv. 12, 13, and free their Hebrew slaves and maidservants (Jer. xxxiv.). The act was of the nature of a solemn covenant with Jehovah, intended to induce him to deliver them from their imminent danger. It may also have had in view the practical aim of increasing the number of loyal defenders to guard the city walls.

205. At this juncture lamentation was temporarily changed to rejoicing by the unexpected departure of the besieging army. The cause was the advance of an Egyptian force under Hophra (Jer. xxxvii. 5). The short respite was regarded by the fanatical people as an omen that they were again to be delivered, as in the days of Hezekiah. Notwithstanding the remonstrances of Jeremiah against their perfidy, the slaves who had been set free were forthwith brought under the old bondage (Jer. xxxiv.). The prophet himself, as

JEREMIAH'S NARROW ESCAPE

he set out for his estate at Anathoth, was arrested, brought before the princes, and charged with attempting to desert to the Chaldeans. His hostile judges, after venting their spite upon him, cast him into a vile prison, where he remained many days, until Zedekiah, alarmed perhaps by the report of the movements of the Chaldean army, secretly summoned him into his presence. In reply to his eager question, Jeremiah declared to the king that he would surely be delivered into the hands of his foe. To those who did not understand the true patriotism which inspired his advice to submit, Jeremiah seemed indeed a traitor to the common cause. The friendship of a king who openly admitted his inability to oppose their will was of no avail to deliver him from the vindictive assault of the princes (Jer. xxxviii.). Not wishing to slay him openly, they let the prophet down into a cistern and left him there to die a miserable death. It was fortunate that there was no water in the cistern, and that Jeremiah had a friend among the heterogeneous crowd which gathered about the king. His deliverer was an Ethiopian by the name of Ebed-meleck ("slave of the king"). Informing his royal master of the danger which threatened the prophet, he was commissioned to go with a band of men to his rescue. During the remainder of the siege, which had meantime been renewed, Jeremiah was under the protection of the royal guard. Again he assured the king, in a private interview, that the only salvation for himself and his capital lay in surrender to the Chaldeans. The irresolute Zedekiah was, however, too weak to oppose his proud princes, who were bent upon continuing the resistance, even though their hopes that Egypt would deliver them had proved utterly futile.

206. Certain passages in Lamentations (ii. 19–22; iv. 10) suggest the horrors of the siege, which lasted a year and a half. Famine drove the Hebrew mothers to such a pitch of madness that they did not hesitate to consume their own children; while it so far weakened the strength of the defenders that in July of 586 B. C. the besiegers were able to force an entrance into the city through the northern wall. Under the cover of night Zedekiah, with his few warriors, fled through the southern gate, down across the barren wilderness of Judea toward the Jordan. The fugitives were overtaken, however, by the Chaldeans on the plain of Jericho; Zedekiah was carried before Nebuchadrezzar at Riblah in Hamath, where he was forced to witness the slaughter of his sons; and then was condemned to lose his eyes and spend the remainder of his days in captivity at Babylon. His nobles, including the leading priests of the Temple, the king's cabinet, the chief military commanders, and sixty of the more prominent elders, were likewise brought before the great king at Riblah and slain. Those who escaped the slaughter at the capture of the city, together with the deserters to the Chaldeans, were carried into exile. Nabuzaradan, an officer of Nebuchadrezzar, was deputed to attend to the destruction of Jerusalem. First it was despoiled of its treasures, the vessels of the Temple, which remained from the first captivity, being among the booty; then all the houses, including the palace and the house of the Lord, were burnt, and the walls of the city torn down. At last Micah's grim prophecy was literally fulfilled: "Jerusalem became heaps, and the mountain of the house as the high places of a forest."

V

THE LAST CHAPTER OF JUDAH'S HISTORY

207. BEFORE the national life of Judah was extinguished entirely, it flashed up in one brilliant, expiring gleam. Not wishing to leave the land utterly desolate, Nebuchadrezzar allowed certain of the poorer Judeans, chiefly vinedressers and shepherds, to remain behind. With them were left a few nobles whose loyalty could be trusted. Over the little state was placed, as governor, Gedaliah, the son of Jeremiah's patron, Ahikam, and the grandson of Josiah's secretary, Shaphan. Jerusalem being destroyed, Mizpah, located on a height a few miles to the north, was selected as the seat of government. Among Gedaliah's stanchest supporters was the prophet Jeremiah. At first he had been carried in chains with other Jewish captives to Ramah (Jer. xl. 1). There a careful investigation was made, by the Chaldean officers, of the record of the prisoners, and judgment meted out according to their deeds. Jeremiah's determined opposition to rebellion was rewarded by giving him the choice of either going with the exiles or remaining with his kinsmen in Judah. Duty, and probably inclination as well, led him to join Gedaliah; for in this noble ruler he recognized one who was in perfect sym-

pathy with his teachings, and who might yet realize what had been impossible while the headstrong princes who had met their fate at Riblah still guided the state.

208. For two bright months (Jer. xli. 1) all went well. Judean fugitives, who had sought refuge among the surrounding peoples, flocked to the standard of the wise Gedaliah. In peace the people turned to agricultural pursuits. Old hopes were being revived, when suddenly all was ruined by an act of superlative treachery. The petty kings of the surrounding nations looked with bitter jealousy upon any prosperity enjoyed by their old rival. Prompted by this feeling, the king of Ammon instigated a certain Jewish prince by the name of Ishmael to kill Gedaliah. Refusing to think any evil of Ishmael, although he had previously been warned of a plot, the generous governor freely extended to him his hospitality, in return for which he received the death-thrust. The few Judeans and the Chaldean soldiers in attendance upon Gedaliah were also slain by the assassin and his followers. Even a band of harmless pilgrims who stopped at Mizpah on their way to the site of the ruined Temple at Jerusalem, did not escape the fiendish perfidy of this base son of the East. With the princesses and the few men of Mizpah who had been spared, Ishmael set out to return to his master, the king of Ammon. On the way, however, he was overtaken by certain followers of the murdered governor, who forced him to abandon his captives and flee for his life.

209. Rejecting Jeremiah's counsel to remain, the little band who survived Ishmael's slaughter fled to Egypt to avoid the vengeance which they feared the

Chaldeans would visit upon them because of the murder of their governor. Perhaps their apprehensions were not without foundation, for, according to Jeremiah lii. 30, there was later still another deportation, whereby seven hundred and forty-five more Judeans were carried to Babylon. In the land of Judah there remained at last only a few humble peasants; all semblance of local government disappeared. Jeremiah was taken by the fugitives into the land of Egypt, where he continued his painful ministry until, according to tradition, he met a martyr's death at the hands of his countrymen. From his latest prophecies it appears that the Egyptian exiles soon relapsed into practical heathenism, retaining only the forms of the worship of Jehovah. That which remained of the real life of the Hebrew people was found among the group of Jewish captives in the land of Babylon, and upon them rested the future of their race and religion. At this point also the history of the Hebrew nation closes, and Jewish history begins.

210. Judah, like the northern kingdom, came to an end from the same causes, and in accordance with the same unchangeable laws which have repeatedly operated in the downfall of other kingdoms. As the prophets so clearly pointed out, religious, social and moral corruption led to the weakening and disintegration of the state. Selfish, inefficient rulers and blind spiritual leaders hastened this process, so that, when the temper of the nation was severely tested by the weight of the heavy yoke of the foreign conqueror, it was unequal to the strain, and in the end Judah's vacillating policy brought down upon it the destructive wrath of Babylon. The individual events in Hebrew history were

analogous to those which entered into the life of other peoples. As has been repeatedly noted, the popular beliefs and the forms in which Jehovah was worshipped were also very similar to those which prevailed among the surrounding Semitic nations. Hebrew history is unique because of the presence and work of its inspired teachers. They moulded its life, interpreted the true significance of its events, and proclaimed the nature, will, and purposes of the Eternal Father, who found in them his willing messengers, and who in turn revealed himself to them as to none of their contemporaries.

211. Hence, while the state was going down to its ruin, the prophetic vision and ideals were always broadening. National experiences, which shook the faith of the masses, constantly opened to the true prophets new and deeper conceptions of Jehovah and of his world plan. While public morals deteriorated, these men, who were in living touch with the Holy One, continued to demand conformity to higher and higher standards of mercy and righteousness. As they were led to perceive the glaring imperfections in the Hebrew commonwealth, they portrayed with ever-increasing definiteness the outlines of the perfect state of the future in which the will of Jehovah should be the supreme law. Gradually they began to realize that their nation as a whole would never attain to the divine ideal. Jeremiah voiced this conclusion, and at the same time opened a new chapter in God's revelation, when he declared, as he sat upon the ruins of Jerusalem, that instead of the old covenant between God and the nation, which had been broken by the people's sins, Jehovah would establish a new and ever-

lasting covenant, inscribed, not in law books, but in the human heart. Then the people would come no more to the priest or prophet to learn the character and will of God, but all would know him, from the least of them even to the greatest (xxxi. 31–34). Old forms would no longer be necessary; even the Ark would be forgotten (iii. 16); for Jehovah himself would cleanse the iniquities of his people and freely pardon. Each man is personally responsible for his own action, and therefore according to his own deeds alone shall he be judged before God (xxxi. 29, 30).

212. Although Jeremiah, with the prophets who had gone before, still looked forward for the realization of these exalted ideals to the time when exile should have done its work of purification and the Jewish race should be restored to its land, he proclaimed in germ the great truth of Christianity, that religion after all is a relation between the loving Father and his individual children. In many ways the message of the weeping prophet is more closely related to the New Testament teaching than that of any other Old Testament writer; but before the supreme truths intrusted to the Hebrew prophets could be imparted to all humanity, they must find personal expression. During the period of the exile this was partially realized in the faithful Israel, who, amidst persecution and doubt, preserved the sacred revelation, and came back to Palestine forever purged of the old idolatry and entirely converted to the teaching of the true prophets. Later Judaism failed, however, to realize fully the prophetic ideals; only in the perfect Son of Man, the Son of the Eternal Father, did the old half-truths find their complete and personal fulfilment. The same God who gradually re-

vealed himself to his people amidst the varied experiences of their history perfected that revelation in the life and work of the Christ, who inaugurated a world-wide, spiritual kingdom, limited to no race or land or forms, and transcending the highest expectations of inspired prophet and psalmist.

APPENDIX

THE AUTHORITIES UPON HEBREW HISTORY

APPENDIX

THE AUTHORITIES UPON HEBREW HISTORY

THE Prophetic period of Hebrew history has evoked from the writers of the past and present a greater volume of literature than any other ancient epoch, except that which immediately followed the beginning of the Christian era. So many and so important have been the new discoveries, however, and so rapid the advances in biblical study, that of the thousands of books which relate to this period, only a very few dating from the preceding decade are still of value even to the technical student. Although the present bibliography is limited to the more recent works, it has been found exceedingly difficult to keep the list of books of reference within practical bounds.

In addition to the books described in the preceding volume of the *History* (pages 209-212), of especial service to the historical student is Schrader's *The Cuneiform Inscriptions and the Old Testament*, in which the author has collected and interpreted the Assyrian inscriptions which throw light upon the Old Testament books. The latest results of Assyriological study are ably presented in Winckler's *Keilinschriftliches Textbuch zum Alten Testament*, which covers the same field. In the new series of the *Records of the Past*, edited by Professor Sayce, is found a translation of many of the more important inscriptions which relate directly or indirectly to the history of the Hebrews. Still more comprehensive, and on the whole more accurate, is the corresponding German work,

Die Keilinschriftliche Bibliothek, prepared under the general editorship of Professor Schrader. It also presents the transliterated text, thus making it possible for those familiar with the Assyrian to verify the suggested translations.

Semitic history has recently been enriched by the second volume of Professor McCurdy's *History, Prophecy, and the Monuments*, which treats of the period of Assyria's greatest power, and consequently of Judah's greatest peril. For a comprehensive survey of Assyrian history Tiele's *Babylonische-Assyrische Geschichte* remains the standard authority. It should, however, be read in connection with Professor Winckler's more recent work, *Geschichte Babyloniens und Assyriens*.

Among a host of recent books dealing with the life and teachings of the Hebrew prophets, W. R. Smith's *Prophets of Israel*, which appears in a new edition with an introduction and a few corrections by Professor Cheyne, continues to be one of the most helpful and inspiring introductions to the Assyrian period of Hebrew history. Kirkpatrick's *The Doctrine of the Prophets* is of great value to the general and technical student alike, since it presents in concise form the characteristic teachings of each prophet, with the date of his activity and the circumstances amidst which he labored. Of the same character is Professor Cornill's little volume on the *Prophets of Israel*, which has recently been translated into English. It is an able popular presentation of the positions of the advanced German school, of which he is a distinguished representative, and will be found exceedingly stimulating.

The list of commentaries upon the different prophetical books has been restricted to a few of the best English works, which present the latest results of biblical scholarship in a form attractive and easily intelligible to all readers. Isaiah is illuminated by the writings of Pro-

AUTHORITIES UPON HEBREW HISTORY   209

fessors Smith and Driver. Both treat his prophecies in their chronological order, and interpret them in their historical setting. Critical questions respecting the date and authorship of the different sections of the Book of Isaiah are considered in detail and from an advanced point of view by Professor Cheyne in his *Introduction to the Book of Isaiah*. For the interpretation of individual passages, the commentaries of Cheyne, Duhm, and Dillmann are the best authorities.

Cheyne's *Jeremiah, His Life and Times* corresponds to the work of Professor Driver upon Isaiah. Although its value to the historical student is somewhat impaired by the presence of a large amount of homiletical material, it is the most useful book on Jeremiah for general reference. The leading commentaries upon Jeremiah's prophecies are those of Cornill, Giesbrecht, and Orelli.

Professor G. A. Smith's *The Book of the Twelve Prophets* is unquestionably the most helpful as well as the latest contribution to the elucidation of the shorter prophetic books. It is characterized by the same excellences as his work on Isaiah. Still more popular is the little volume in the *Men of the Bible Series* by Canon Farrar on *The Minor Prophets*. For the interpretation of individual passages, Orelli's *The Book of the Twelve Minor Prophets* is valuable. Students of the German will consult with great profit Wellhausen's *Die Kleinen Propheten* in *Skizzen und Vorarbeiten*.

Within its special field, the *Messianic Prophecy* of Riehm is the most lucid and suggestive introduction. For the classification and epitomization of the different passages the *Messianic Prophecy* by Professor Briggs is exceedingly useful, and largely supplants the older and more conservative *Old Testament Prophecy* by Orelli.

BOOKS OF REFERENCE

LITERATURE

Abbreviations

Dr. L. O. T.* . . Driver — Introduction to the Literature of the Old Testament (6th edition).
R. P. . . . . Records of the Past, New Series, I–VI. 1892.
Sch. C. I. O. T. . Schrader — The Cuneiform Inscriptions and the Old Testament, I., II. (Eng. transl. 1885).
Corn. E. A. T. . . Cornill — Einleitung in das Alte Testament (2te Aufl.) 1892.
K. B. . . . . Keilinschriftliche Bibliothek, I.–III. 1889–1892).

HISTORY

Kitt. H. H. . . . . Kittel — History of the Hebrews, I., II. (Eng. transl. 1895, 1896).
Mc. H. P. M. . . . McCurdy — History, Prophecy, and the Monuments, I., II.
Re. H. P. I. . . . . Renan — History of the People of Israel, II., III. 1891.
Ew. H. I. . . . . . Ewald — History of Israel, IV. (Eng. transl. 1883–1885).
St. G. V. I. . . . Stade — Geschichte des Volkes Israel, I. 1887.
Winck. G. I. . . . Winckler — Geschichte Israels in Einzeldarstellungen, I. 1895.
Tiele, B. A. G. . . Tiele — Babylonische-Assyrische Geschichte, I., II. 1886, 1888.

PROPHECY

Abbreviations

Sm. P. I.	W. R. Smith — The Prophets of Israel (new edition), 1897.
Kirk. D. P.	Kirkpatrick — The Doctrine of the Prophets, 1892.
Corn. P. I.	Cornill — The Prophets of Israel, 1895.
Sm. B. I.	G. A. Smith — The Book of Isaiah, I. 1890.
Dr. I.	Driver — Isaiah, His Life and Times, 1888.
Cheyne, J.	Cheyne — Jeremiah, His Life and Times, 1890.
Gieseb. B. J. . . .	Giesebrecht — Das Buch Jeremiah, 1894.
Sm. B. T. P. . . .	G. A. Smith — The Book of the Twelve Prophets, I., II. 1896, 1898.
Far. M. P.	Farrar — The Minor Prophets, 1895.

RELIGION

Schultz, O. T. T. .	Schultz — Old Testament Theology, I., II. (Eng. transl. 1892).
Kuen. R. I. . . .	Kuenen — The Religion of Israel.
Mont. R. A. H. .	Montefiore — The Religion of the Ancient Hebrews, 1892.
Dill. H. A. T. . .	Dillmann — Handbuch der Alttestamentlichen Theologie, 1895.
Smend, A. T. . . .	Smend — Alttestamentliche Theologie, 1893.

ANTIQUITIES AND HISTORICAL GEOGRAPHY.

Sm. H. G. H. L. .	G. A. Smith — The Historical Geography of the Holy Land, 1894.
Benz. H. A.	Benzinger — Hebräische Archäologie, 1894.

ENCYCLOPÆDIAS

En. B.	Encyclopædia Britannica.
Hast. D. B.	Hastings — A Dictionary of the Bible, 1898.

REFERENCES

Part I. — THE PRE-ASSYRIAN PERIOD OF HEBREW HISTORY

I.

THE HISTORICAL SOURCES FOR THE PERIOD

I. Kgs. xii.–II. Kgs. iii.; II. Chrs. x. 1–xxii. 9; Dr. L. O. T.⁕ 193–196, 516–535; Sch. C. I .O. T.,.I. 177–195; R. P., II. 194–203, IV. 42–71; Sm. P. I. 376–378; En. B. XIV. 85, 86; Hast. D. B., I. 395, 396; Kitt. H. H., II. 205–216, 224–233; St. G. V. I. 73–79; K. B., I. 170–174.

II.

THE CHRONOLOGY OF THE TWO KINGDOMS

Sm. P. I. 144–151, 403–405; Mc. H. P. M., II. 420–423 ; R. P., II. 110–127, 207, 208 ; Hast. D. B., I. 400–403; Ew. H. I., IV. 20–22, 295–299; Sch. C. I. O. T. II.,161–199; Kitt. H. H., II. 234–240 ; St. G. V. I. 88–99; Tiele, B. A. G., I. 92–99.

III

THE DIVISION OF THE HEBREW KINGDOM

I. Kgs. xii. 1–24; Mc. H. P. M., I. 252–254; En. B. XIII. 406, Corn. H P., I. 95, 96; Re. H. P. I., II. 149–154 ; Mont. R. A. H. 83–86; Kitt. H. H., II. 241–246 ; St. G. V. I. 344–349; Dill. H. A. T. 162–164.

IV

RESOURCES AND ORGANIZATION OF THE TWO KINGDOMS.

I. Kgs. xii. 25–32; xiii. 33, 34 ; Sm. H. G. H. L. 257–364 Mc. H. P. M., I. 316–322 ; Ew. H. I., IV. 1–20; Re. H. P. I., II. 155–165; Dill. H. A. T. 164–170.

V

POLITICAL EVENTS IN ISRAEL AND JUDAH

I. Kgs. xvi. 1-xvi. 34; xx. 1-43; xxii. 1-53; II. Kgs. iii. 1-27; Mc. H. P. M., I. 254-286; Corn. H. P. I. 97-108; En. B. XIII. 406; Ew. H. I., IV. 23-59, 71-78; Re. H. P. I., II. 206-219, 243-260; Sch. C. I. O. T., I. 177-195; Sm. H. G. H. L. 345, 346; Hast. D. B., I. 51-53; Kitt. H. H., II. 246-261, 270-277; Dill. H. A. T. 170-172; St. G. V. I. 349-357, 519-524, 527-541; Tiele, B. A. G., I. 185-192; Winck. G. I. 133-155, 160-165, 175-177.

VI

THE RELIGIOUS CRISIS IN ISRAEL, AND THE WORK OF ELIJAH

I. Kgs. xvii. 1-xix. 21; xxi. 1-29; II. Kgs. i. 1-ii. 25; Sm. P. I. 72-85; Corn. P. I. 29-36; Ew. H. I., IV. 63-71, 101-113; En. B. VIII. 134-136, XIII. 407; Mont. R. A. H. 89-96; Sm. B. T. P., I. 20-30; Kuen. R. I., I. 343-357; Re. H. P. I., II. 220-242; Hast. D. B., I. 687-691; Smend, A. T. 152-159; Dill. H. A. T. 172, 173; St. G. V. I. 524-527.

PART II. — THE ASSYRIAN PERIOD OF ISRAEL'S HISTORY

I

THE HISTORICAL SOURCES AND CHRONOLOGY

II. Kgs. iv.-xvii.; Amos; Hosea; Dr. L. O. T.* 300-307, 313-318, 196, 197; R. P., IV. 86-95, V. 115-128; En. B. XIV. 86; Sm. B. T. P. I. 61-72, 211-226; Sm. P. I. 405-407; Sch. C. I. O. T., I. 196-277; Kitt. H. H., II. 216-223; St. G. V. I. 558-561; K. B. I. 174-193, II. 2-80.

II

THE REVOLUTION OF JEHU

II. Kgs. ix. 1-x. 31; Sm. P. I. 85-87; En. B. XIII. 407, 408, VIII. 140-142; Corn. H. P. I. 108-114; Ew. H. I., IV. 96-101;

Kuen. R. I., II. 261-274; Re. H. P. I., II. 261-274; Schultz, O. T. T. I. 235-246; Sch. C. I. O. T., I. 196-201; Kitt. H. H., II. 278-282; St. G. V. I. 541-545.

III

ISRAEL UNDER THE RULE OF THE HOUSE OF JEHU

II. Kgs. vi. 8-vii. 20; x. 32-36; xiii. 1-25; xiv. 8-29; Mc. H. P. M., I. 286-301, 308-310; Corn. H. P. I. 117-119; Sm. P. I. 90-93; Ew. H. I., IV. 114-123; Re. H. P. I., II. 340-349; Sch. C. I. O. T., I. 202-208; Kitt. H. H., II. 289-296; St. G. V. I. 562-566; Tiele, B. A. G. I. 193-216.

IV

THE PROPHETS AMOS AND HOSEA

Sm. P. I. 120-190; Sm. B. T. P. I. 73-354; Kirk. D. P. 88-140; Corn. P. I. 37-55; Far. M. P. 35-102; Kuen. R. I., I. 188-212; Re. H. P. I., II. 350-403; Mont. R. A. H. 119-139; En. B. XIII. 410; XII. 295-298; Mc. H. P. M., I. 344-346; Ew. H. I., IV. 126-133; Kitt. H. H., II. 312-328; Smend, A. T. 159-203; St. G. V. I. 570-582.

V

SOCIETY AND MORALS IN ISRAEL

Sm. P. I. 87-89, 93-96; Sm. B. T. P., I. 31-43; Kirk. D. P. 84-88; Mc. H. P. M., I. 310, 311, 337-343; Mont. R. A. H. 112-118; Kitt. H. H., II. 296-311; Ew. H. I., IV. 124-126; Dill. H. A. T. 174, 175.

VI

POPULAR AND PROPHETIC RELIGION

Sm. P. I. 97-102; Sm. B. T. P., I. 44-58; Far. M. P. 1-15, 28-34; Kuen. P. I., I. 35-85; Schultz, O. T. T., I. 220-230; Mont. R. A. H. 97-105; En. B. XIII. 411; St. G. V. I. 428-517, 550-558, 582-585; Winck. G. I. 65-70, 82-86.

VII

THE DECLINE AND FALL OF ISRAEL

II. Kgs. xv. 8-31; xvii. 1-41; Mc. H. P. M., I. 323-337, 351-358, 372-397; En. B. XIII. 412; Corn. H. P. I. 122, 123, 125; Ew. H. I., IV. 148-166; Re. H. P. I., II. 425-444; Sch. C. I. O. T., I. 219-254, 257-268; Kitt. H. H., II. 332-335, 337-339, 348-354; St. G. V. I. 598-601: Tiele, B. A. G., I. 217-240; Winck. G. I. 167-171.

VIII

THE RÔLE OF ISRAEL IN THE WORLD'S HISTORY

Mc. H. P. M., I. 397-401; Sch. C. I. O. T., I. 268-277; Corn. H. P. I. 126-130; Re. H. P. I., II. 445-455; Kitt H. H., II. 353-354; St. G. V. I. 601, 602.

PART III. — THE ASSYRIAN PERIOD OF JUDAH'S HISTORY

I

THE HISTORICAL SOURCES AND CHRONOLOGY

II. Kgs. xi.-xxi.; II. Chrs. xxii. 10-xxxiii. 25; Isa. i.-xxxix; Micah; Dr. L. O. T.[6] 196, 197, 204-226, 325-334; R. P., I. 168-175, VI. 80-101; Sch. C. I. O. T., I. 277-310, II. 1-43; Sm. B. T. P., I. 357-374; Kirk. D. P. 225-231; Sm. P. I. 210-217, 404, 405, 414-423; Mc. H. P. M., II. 248-252; Kitt. H. H., II. 208-223; K. B., II. 25-33, 80-152.

II

FROM ATHALIAH TO AHAZ

II. Kgs. xi. 1-xii. 21; xiv. 1-22; xv. 1-7; II. Chrs. xxii. 10-xxvii. 9; Mc. H. P. M., I. 301-308, 312-315, 347-350; Sm. P. I. 191-199; Dr. I. 5-14; Ew. H. I., IV. 134-146; Corn. H. P. I. 115-117, 120-122; Sch. C. I. O. T., I. 208-215; Kitt. H. H., II. 282-289; Dill. H. A. T. 175-177; St. G. V. I. 545-549, 566-570; Winck. G. I. 177-179; Benz. H. A. 410-414.

III

THE CRISIS OF 734 B. C.

II. Kgs. xvi.; II. Chrs. xxviii.; Isa. v. 1-x. 4; Mc. H. P. M., I. 315, 316, 366-371; Sm. P. I. 217-224, 235-278; Sm. I., L 3-130; Dr. I. 1-4, 15-42; Kirk. D. P. 141-152, 158-160; Corn. H. P. I. 123-125; Ew. H. I., IV. 166-172; Sch. C. I. O. T., L 255-257; Kitt. H. H., II. 339-348; St. G. V. I. 585-598.

IV

SOCIETY AND RELIGION IN JUDAH

Isa. ii.; iii. 1-iv. 1; v.; Micah i-iii.; Mc. H. P. M., I. 359-366; II., 252-257; Sm. P. I. 199-205; Sm. B. T. P., I. 375-399; Kirk. D. P. 152-158, 201-225; Far. M. P. 124-140; En. B. XIII. 412, 413; Kuen. R. I., I. 374-390; Ew. H. I., IV. 146-148; Re. H. P. I., II. 416-424; Dill. H. A. T. 175-178; Schultz, O. T. T., L 230-235, 246, 290; Winck. G. I. 87-90.

V

THE GREAT INVASION OF SENNACHERIB

II. Kgs. xviii.-xx.; II. Chrs. xxix.-xxxii.; Isa. xx.; xxii. 15-25; xxviii.-xxxii.; x. 5-xi. 9; xiv. 24-27; xvii. 12-14; xviii.; xxii. 1-14; xxxvi.-xxxvii.; Micah iv.; v.; Sm. P. I. 279-356; Dr. I. 43-83; Sm. I., I. 151-204, 306-374; Kirk. D. P. 161-168; Mc. H. P. M., II. 258-321, 428-431; Corn. H. P. I. 130-136; Re. H. P. I., III., 79-93; Ew. H. I., IV. 172-190; Sch. C. I. O. T., I. 277-310, II., 1-43, 82-103; Sm. H. G. H. L. 157-160; Kitt. H. H., II. 355-370; St. G. V. I. 603-624; Tiele, B. A. G. 244-325.

VI

THE WORK AND TEACHINGS OF ISAIAH

Sm. P. I. 205-210, 224-234, 424; Sm. I. 131-150; Dr. I. 107-116; Kirk. D. P. 169-196; Corn. P. I. 56-70; Schultz, O. T. T., I. 290-297; Mont. R. A. H. 139-160; Smend, A. T. 203-227; Winck. G. I. 97, 98.

VII

THE REACTIONARY REIGN OF MANASSEH

II. Kgs. xxi.; II. Chrs. xxxiii.; Micah. vi. 1-vii. 6.; Mc. H. P. M., II. 377-390; Sm. P. I. 356-373; Corn. P. I. 71-79; Sm. B. T. P. 419-434; Mont. R. A. H. 161-173; Sch. C. I. O. T., II. 53-59; Ew. H. I., IV. 206-225; Corn. H. P. I. 136, 137; Re. H. P. I., III. 103-113; Kuen. R. I., II. 1-6; Kitt. H. H., II. 370-379; Dill. H. A. T. 178, 179; St. G. V. I. 624-641; Tiele, B. A. G. 325-351; Winck. G. I. 98-107.

Part IV. — THE BABYLONIAN PERIOD OF JUDAH'S HISTORY

I

THE HISTORICAL SOURCES

II. Kgs. xxii.-xxv.; II. Chrs. xxxiv.-xxxvi.; Zephaniah; Nahum; Habakkuk; Jeremiah; Obadiah; Ezek. i.-xxiv.; Dr. L. O. T.⁶ 197-200, 247-286, 318-320, 334-343; Sch. C. I. O. T., II. 43-52; Kirk. D. P. 235-246, 280-285; Gieseb. J. xiv.-xix.

II

THE GREAT REFORMATION UNDER JOSIAH

II. Kgs. xxii. 1-xxiii. 30; II. Chrs. xxxiv-xxxv.; Zephaniah; Jer. i.-vi.; xi. 1-8; Mc. H. P. M., II. 391-402: Corn. P. I. 80-99; En. B. XIII. 415, XXI. 575-577; Cheyne, J. 1-101; Far. M. P. 153-158; Kirk. D. P. 253-263, 296-298; Mont. R. A. H. 173-195; Corn. H. P. I. 137, 138; Kuen. R. I., II. 7-40; Re. H. P. I., III. 114-184; Ew. H. I., IV. 226-240; Kitt. H. H., II. 379-385; Smend, A. T. 227-233, 263-302; St. G. V. I. 641-671; Winck. G. I. 107-111, 185, 186; Benz. H. A. 389-393, 418.

III

JUDAH AND THE NEW WORLD POWERS

II. Kgs. xxiii. 31–xxiv. 17; II. Chrs. xxxvi. 1–10; Habakkuk; Nahum; Jer. xxii. 1–12; xxvi.; vii.–ix.; x. 17–25; xi. 9–xii. 6; xxv.; xxxvi.; xiv.–xx.; xxxv.; xii. 7–xiii. 27; xxii. 13–30; Mc. H. P. M., II. 402–414; Corn. P. I. 99–102; Cheyne, 102–164; Far. M. P. 141–152, 159–174; Kirk D. P. 246–252, 264–280; Schultz, O. T. T., I. 300–307; Mont. R. A. H. 195–204; Sch. C. I. O. T., II. 43–47; Corn. H. P. I. 138–142; Kuen. R. I., II. 41–47, 52–65; Ew. H. I., IV. 240–264; Re. H. P. I., III. 210–242; Kitt. H. H., II. 385–400; Smend, A. T. 233–252; St. G. V. I. 671–681; Tiele, B. A. G. 400–427.

IV

JEREMIAH AND THE FALL OF JERUSALEM

II. Kgs. xxiv. 18–xxv. 21; II. Chrs. xxxvi. 11–21; Obadiah; Jer. xxiv.; xxvii.–xxxiv.; l.; li.; xxi. 1–10; xxiii.; xxxvii.–xxxix.; Ezek. i.–xxiv.; Corn. P. I. 102–107; Cheyne, J. 165–181; Kirk. D. P. 298–310, 321–345; Schultz, O. T. T., I. 307–310; Mont. R. A. H. 204–208; Sch. C. I. O. T., II. 47–52; Ew. H. I., IV. 264–274; Re. H. P. I., III. 243–274; Kitt. H. H., II. 385–395; Smend, A. T. 252–262; St. G. V. I. 681–694; Tiele, B. A. G. 427–441; Winck. G. I. 109–113, 188, 189; Gieseb. J. v.–xiv.

V

THE LAST CHAPTER OF JUDAH'S HISTORY

II. Kgs. xxv. 22–30; Jer. xl.–xliv.; lii.; Cheyne, J. 182–205; Kirk. D. P. 310–320; Mont. R. A. H. 208–221; Ew. H. I., IV. 274–276; Re. H. I., III. 282–308; Dill. H. A. T. 180–183; St. G. V. I. 694–703.

INDEXES

INDEX OF NAMES AND SUBJECTS

ABEL, city of, 36, 101.
Abel-Meholah, 61.
Abiathar, 175.
Abijam, 10, 36, 46.
Absalom, 19, 26.
Achbor, 177.
Acts of the Kings of Israel, 9.
Adoram, 23.
Ahab, policy of, 39, 48, 49, 63, 87; court of, 70; wars of, 14, 15, 37-42, 64; tyranny of, 53, 54; relations to Elijah, 47, 48, 50-53; death of, 42; family of, 44, 65, 66, 121.
Ahaz, 102, 113, 114, 116, 117, 119, 126, 128, 130-133, 135, 139, 141, 153, 161.
Ahaziah of Israel, 15, 42, 48.
Ahaziah of Judah, 44, 67, 120.
Ahijah, 20.
Ahikam, 177, 187, 199.
Amaziah, King of Judah, 75, 117, 122-124.
Amaziah, high priest at Bethel, 82, 83, 89, 93.
Ammon, 102, 145, 194, 196, 200.
Ammonites, 27.
Amon, 114, 164, 172, 173.
Amos, date of, 13, 79; call of, 86-82; character of, 8, 79, 80; mission of, 6, 81; sermons of, 33, 83, 85, 123; teachings of, 68, 86-94, 109, 135, 151, 174; theology of, 94-96, 109, 152.
Amos, Book of, 58.
Anathoth, 175, 187, 197.
Aphek, 40-42.
Arabah, 76.
Arabia, 102, 125, 134.

Arabs, 27, 28, 107, 125, 143.
Arameans, 28, 40, 41, 44, 49, 50, 65, 70-77, 95, 114, 115, 143.
Ark, 32, 129, 203.
Armenians, 76.
Arnon, 72.
Arpad, 105.
Asa, 4, 27, 36, 37, 43, 46.
Asaiah, 177.
Ashdod, 142, 147.
Asherim, 157, 160, 186, 194.
Askelon, 101, 145.
Assyria, 14, 15, 45, 59, 60, 72, 74-77, 95, 99-104, 115, 119, 123, 126, 127, 130-134, 141-150, 155, 160-162, 168, 173, 174, 183.
Assyrians, chronology of, 13, 14, 39, 43, 59, 60, 71, 116; invasions of, 28, 98-104, 130-133, 145-150; overthrow of, 154, 168, 176.
Athaliah, 44, 48, 116, 117, 120, 121.
Avva, 106.
Azariah of Israel, 116.
Azariah (Uzziah) of Judah, 99, 117, 124-126, 128, 134.

BAAL, 48, 50-52, 54, 62, 65, 121, 137, 177, 186.
Baalism, 46, 65, 68, 69, 90, 121, 137, 138.
Baasha, 4, 36, 37.
Babylon, 29, 106, 107, 118, 143, 170, 191-197, 201.
Babylonians, 107, 183.
Barak, 18.
Baruch, 170, 190.
Benhadad I., 36, 37, 39-41, 64.
Benhadad II., 70, 73.

INDEX OF NAMES AND SUBJECTS

Benhadad III., 78.
Benjamin, 26, 27.
Bethel, city of, 32, 62, 82, 83, 108; royal sanctuary at, 5, 32, 33, 177.
Bethlehem, 32, 79.
Bethshean, 61.
Bethshemesh, 75, 124.
Bidkar, 67.
Book of the Kings of Israel and Judah, 9, 10.
Bozrah, 123.

CALF worship, 32-34, 96.
Canaan, 16, 17, 28, 45.
Canaanites, 51.
Caphtor, 95.
Carchemish, 168, 188, 190.
Carmel, Mount, 52.
Chaldeans, 168, 169, 188, 190, 193, 194, 197-201.
Chebar, 170, 193.
Chemosh, 177.
Cherubim, 32, 129.
Christ, the, 54, 158, 204.
Chronicler, the, 8-11, 125, 147.
Chronicles, Second Book of, 7-11, 17.
Chronicles of the Kings of Judah, 5.
Chronology, biblical, 6, 12-15, 59, 60, 116-119; Assyrian, 13, 14, 59, 60, 116, 117.
Chemosh, 38, 92.
Commerce, 87.
Covenant, 177, 202, 203.
Cuthah, 106.
Cyaxares, 183.

DAMASCUS, 15, 29, 36-39, 41-43, 70-77, 87, 99, 101, 102, 105, 122-124, 126, 127, 131-133.
Dan, city of, 36; sanctuary of, 32.
David, 18, 19, 22-24, 26, 30, 35, 36, 39, 76, 120, 128, 154, 181.
Dead Sea, 27, 42, 76, 123.
Deborah, 18.
Deportations, 193, 198, 201.
Deuteronomic editor, 167.
Deuteronomy, Book of, date of, 162, 163, 167, 196; authorship of, 162-164, 178, 179; finding of, 164, 176, 177; teaching of, 63, 163, 164, 181; influence of, 177-182.

Disruption, causes of, 16-22, 47; act of, 22, 23; effects of, 24, 25.
Divination, 63, 178.

EBAL, Mount, 35.
Ebed-melech, 197.
Edom, 27, 75, 102, 123, 142, 145, 170.
Edomites, 44, 72, 115, 123, 127.
Egypt, 15, 28, 32, 36, 59, 74, 95, 97, 100-105, 115, 131, 142, 144, 145, 148, 149, 155, 160, 173, 184, 187, 188, 191, 193, 196, 197, 200.
Elah, 37.
Elam, 107.
Elamites, 107, 143.
Elath, 114, 123, 125, 127, 134.
Eli, 175.
Elijah, stories respecting, 6, 7, 113; character of, 51, 52, 57, 60, 61, 64; relations to Ahab, 47, 48; teachings of, 32, 67, 69, 121; work of, 52, 53, 54, 66, 109; calling of Elisha, 61.
Elisha, stories respecting, 6, 7, 57, 73, 114; call of, 61; teachings of, 32; character of, 61, 62; work of, 62-67, 74, 109; influence of, 73, 74.
Eltekeh, 145.
Ephesus, 52.
Ephraim, land of, 17, 30, 63, 99, 101.
Ephraim, tribe of, 18, 29.
Esarhaddon, 107.
Esdraelon, plain of, 29, 30, 39, 67, 72, 101, 102, 106, 184.
Ethbaal, 48, 52.
Ethiopia, 103, 142.
Ehiopians, 115, 197.
Euphrates, 184, 185, 188.
Ezekiel, the prophet, 12, 119, 195, 196.
Ezekiel, Book of, 170.
Ezion-Geber, 44.

FEASTS, 33.

GALILEE, Sea of, 37.
Gath, 72, 122, 125, 142.
Gaza, 101, 141, 147.
Geba, 27, 37.
Gedaliah, 199, 200.
Gehazi, 63.
Gerizim, 35, 107.

INDEX OF NAMES AND SUBJECTS

Gibbethon, 36, 37.
Gideon, 17, 18, 35.
Gilboa, 18.
Gilead, 51, 59.
Gilgal, 31, 62.
Gomer, 84.

HABAKKUK, the prophet, 188, 189.
Habakkuk, Book of, 168.
Habor, 106.
Halah, 106.
Hamath, 76, 99, 105–107, 126, 198.
Hananiah, 195.
Hazael, 70–73, 122.
Hazor, 101.
Hermon, Mount, 71.
Herodotus, 171, 173.
Hexateuch, 108.
Hezekiah, 118, 119, 131, 135, 138, 140–143, 147–150, 157–159, 162, 163, 187, 196.
Hiel, 39.
High places, 178, 180.
High priest, 176.
Hilkiah, 176, 177.
Hinnom, 177.
Hiram of Tyre, 99.
Historical sources, 3–11, 57–60, 113–119, 167–171.
Hittites, 74, 106.
Hophra, 196.
Hosea, the prophet, nationality of, 83; call of, 83, 84; teachings of, 85, 89–94, 100, 132, 151; theology of, 94–97, 109, 110, 152; work of, 128, 130.
Hosea, Book of, 58, 109.
Hoshea, 60, 101–103.
Huldah, 177.

IBLEAM, 67.
Ijon, 36, 101.
Immanuel, 131.
India, 125, 134.
Inscriptions, Assyrian, 13, 59, 74, 96, 116, 124, 126, 145; Babylonian, 149, 171; Egyptian, 11, 15; Hebrew, 141; Phoenician, 11.
Isaiah, training of, 128, 129; call of, 129, 130; teachings of, 114, 130–133, 135–137, 143, 144, 149, 159, 179, 186; theology of, 138–140, 152, 153;

Messianic ideals of, 153–155; work of, 113, 149, 151, 155–158.
Isaiah, Book of, 114–116.
Ishmael, 200.
Israel, politics of, 4, 14, 15, 17, 24, 28, 31, 33, 35–44, 47–54, 70–77, 86–91, 98–110.
Issachar, tribe of, 36.

JEBUS, 17.
Jehoahaz of Israel, 72.
Jehoahaz of Judah, 169, 184, 185.
Jehoiada, 44, 120–122.
Jehoiakim, 168, 169, 185–192.
Jehoiakin, 192, 193.
Jehoram (or Joram) of Israel, 15, 42, 44, 43, 65, 66.
Jehoram of Judah, 44, 123.
Jehoshaphat, 4, 42–44, 46, 49, 63.
Jehovah, popular conceptions of, 24, 92–94, 107–110, 137, 138, 160, 161; symbols of, 32; crisis in religion of, 50, 51; Elijah's conception of, 54, 69; Amos's and Hosea's conception of, 94–97; Isaiah's couception of, 138–140, 152–155; prophetic conception of, 202–204.
Jehu, 14, 15, 39, 43, 44, 54, 57–60, 64–73, 78, 116, 120.
Jeremiah, date of, 12, 119, 168, 169, 175; call of, 175; fortunes of, 170, 176, 186, 187, 190–193, 195–197; character of, 175; sermons of, 170, 171, 181; teachings of, 181, 187–189, 191, 192, 194–197, 202–204; death of, 201.
Jeremiah, Book of, 168.
Jericho, 39, 62, 198.
Jeroboam I., 4, 10, 15, 20, 23, 30–34, 36–38.
Jeroboam II., 6, 58, 59, 75, 76, 78, 79, 82, 83, 86, 89, 92, 98, 104, 126.
Jerusalem, 12, 22, 24, 26, 29–31, 33, 36, 72, 115, 118, 124, 126, 133, 134, 142, 144–149, 152, 154, 157–159, 169, 171, 174–179, 186, 187, 191–193, 196, 202.
Jews, 69, 106.
Jezebel, 48, 49, 52, 62, 63, 65, 67.
Jezreel, 39, 48, 53, 65–68.
Joab, 19.

INDEX OF NAMES AND SUBJECTS

Joash of Israel, 75, 76, 117, 124.
Joash of Judah, 44, 113, 121, 122, 171.
Job, Book of, 92.
Jonadab, 191, 192.
Jonah, 79.
Jordan, 11, 29, 39, 51, 66, 102, 198.
Joseph, house of, 26.
Joshua, 18.
Josiah, 5, 158, 164, 168, 172, 173, 176–178, 180, 181, 184, 185, 190, 199.
Jotham, 117, 125, 126, 135.
Judah, politics of, 4, 14, 15, 17–20, 24, 26–30, 33, 36–38, 47, 49, 75, 76, 101, 120–126, 141–150, 183–204.
Judaism, 158, 203.
Judges, Book of, 8, 16, 109, 181.

Karkar, 15, 41.
Karnak, 36.
Kedesh, 101.
Kidron, 177.
King, Hebrew, 30, 31, 47.
Kings, First Book of, 3–6, 13, 17, 22, 46, 47, 181.
Kings, Second Book of, 3, 6, 7, 17, 57, 58, 74, 109, 113, 114, 167, 181.
Kings, Midrash of the Book of, 9.
Kirjath-jearim, 187.

Lachish, 124, 149.
Lamentations, Book of, 198.
Lebanon, Mount, 76, 154.
Libnah, 44, 149.
Literature of the Old Testament, 181, 182.

Manasseh, King, 114, 116, 119, 159–161, 162–164, 167, 172, 179, 186.
Manasseh, tribe of, 13, 30.
Mareshah, 43.
Mattan, 121.
Medes, 106, 168, 183.
Meander, 52.
Mediterranean Sea, 75, 99, 101, 145, 167, 173.
Megiddo, 67, 184.
Menahem, 60, 98–100.
Merodach-Baladan, 118, 143, 145.
Mesha, 11, 42, 43, 92.
Mesopotamia, 106, 143.
Messianic ideals, 153–155, 159.

Micah, the prophet, 125, 136, 137, 138, 151, 154, 156, 157, 187, 198.
Micah, Book of, 116, 119, 159–161.
Micaiah, 49, 50, 64.
Midrash, of the Book of Kings, 9, 10; of the prophet Iddo, 10.
Millo, 122.
Mizpah, 27, 31, 37, 199, 200.
Moab, 11, 38, 42, 43, 72, 79, 92, 102, 142, 145, 194.
Moabites, 27, 42, 43, 72, 76, 92.
Moabite stone, 11, 43, 92.
Moloch, 160, 177.
Moresheth, 125, 156, 181.
Moses, 32, 138, 157, 163, 164.

Nabopolassar, 183, 188.
Naboth, 53, 65, 67.
Nadab, 36.
Nahum, the prophet, 176, 183.
Nahum, Book of, 167, 168.
Nazirite, 51.
Nebuchadrezzar, 169, 171, 188, 189, 193–199.
Nebuzaradan, 198.
Necho, 184, 185.
Nile, 99, 141, 149, 185.
Nineveh, 148, 168, 184, 188.

Obadiah, Book of, 170.
Omri, 11, 37–39, 41, 43, 44, 46, 54, 66, 68, 70, 75, 98.
Ophir, 44.
Orientalism, 21, 23, 53, 54.
Orontes, 185.
Osorkon II., 43.

Padi, 144, 146.
Palestine, 59, 76, 99, 101, 103, 105, 107, 115, 123, 134, 145, 149, 167, 173, 191, 193, 203.
Pashur, 192.
Pekah, 60, 100, 101, 116, 127, 130, 132, 133.
Pekahiah, 60, 100.
Penuel, 35.
Philistia, 75, 144, 147.
Philistines, 18, 27, 72, 95, 115, 125, 127, 133.
Phœnicia, 144, 145.

INDEX OF NAMES AND SUBJECTS

Phœnicians, 48, 52, 62.
Phraortes, 168.
Priests, of Judah, 30, 120-122, 178, 180; of Israel, 32, 33, 47, 139.
Prophetic guilds, 62-64.
Prophets, 20, 21, 30, 46, 47, 49-51, 78-80, 85, 136-140, 143, 155, 156, 160-162, 174, 194, 202, 203.
Proverbs, 108.
Proverbs, Book of, 142, 182.
Psalms, 108, 182.
Pul, 98, 99.

RAMAH, 27, 36, 199.
Ramman-nirari, 74, 75.
Ramoth Gilead, 15, 42, 49, 65.
Raphia, 141.
Recabites, 51, 191, 192.
Recorder, 5.
Red Sea, 43, 123, 125.
Reforms, 140, 169, 172-181, 184.
Rehoboam, 10, 21-23, 35, 36, 46.
Religion, of Israel, 31-34, 36, 46; of Samaritans, 107, 108; of Judah, 137-140, 158-162, 177-181.
Revolution of Jehu, 65-69.
Rezon, 39, 99, 100, 116, 127, 130, 132.
Riblah, 185, 198, 200.
Rome, 29.

SAMARIA, 38, 40, 42, 48, 59, 67, 68, 73, 100, 103-107, 115, 116, 118, 119, 132, 141, 156.
Samaritans, 58, 106-108.
Samuel, the prophet, 18, 62, 64.
Samuel, First Book of, 3, 109, 181.
Sargon, 59, 104-107, 115, 141, 143-145.
Saul, 18, 26.
Scythians, 167, 168, 173, 183.
Sela, 123, 134.
Sennacherib, 113, 115, 116, 118, 145-150, 154, 158.
Sepharvaim, 106.
Shabaka, 141.
Shallum, 98.
Shalmaneser II., 14, 41, 59, 70, 71.
Shalmaneser III., 76.
Shalmaneser IV., 59, 102-104.
Shamshi-Ramman II., 71, 75.

Shaphan, 177, 187, 190, 199.
Sheva, 23.
Shechem, 35, 38, 107.
Shishak II., 11, 15, 36.
Shiloh, 31, 186.
Sidon, 71, 75, 144, 145.
Siloam, 141.
Simeon, tribe of, 29.
Society, in Israel, 86-89; in Judah, 134-137, 201.
Solomon, 19-24, 30-33, 36, 39, 46, 48, 76, 87, 121, 134, 157, 175, 177, 185.
Song of Songs, 108, 109.
Sons of the prophets, 63-65.
Syria, 101, 105, 106, 133, 142.

TEKOA, 79.
Teman, 123.
Temple, building of, 19, 121; influence of, 29, 34, 46, 119, 180; precincts of, 177, 192; equipment of, 32, 36, 133, 198; treasure of, 122; plunder of, 36, 124, 148, 193-198; guard of, 120; cleansing of, 177; service of, 160, 161, 186; repair of, 113, 121, 122, 126, 139, 176.
Tibni, 37.
Tiglath-Pileser III., 59, 60, 98-102, 117, 132, 133, 153.
Tigris, 99, 106, 123.
Tirhakah, 144, 145, 149.
Tirzah, 4, 35, 37, 38, 98.
Tophet, 177.
Tyre, 39, 48, 71, 75, 99, 194, 196.

URIAH, the prophet, 187.
Uzziah (Azariah), 13, 114, 124-126.

VIRGIN'S FOUNT, 130, 141.

WIZARDS, 63, 132, 178.
Worship, 131.

ZECHARIAH, the king, 98.
Zechariah, the prophet, 13.
Zedekiah, 169, 194, 197, 198.
Zephaniah, the prophet, 167, 173-177.
Zephaniah, Book of, 167, 168.
Zerah, 43.
Zimri, 4, 37, 67.

INDEX OF REFERENCES

TO

BIBLICAL AND EXTRA-BIBLICAL SOURCES

	Page		Page		Page
LEVITICUS.		**I. KINGS.**		iii. 11	61
xix. 2	152	i.-xi.	3	iv.	57
xx. 7, 26	152	i. 35	17	iv.-xvii.	57
		iv. 3	5	v. 1	62
DEUTERONOMY.		iv. 20, 25.	17	iv. 1-viii. 15.	57
vii. 6	179	iv. 38, 41	62	iv. 1-7, 38, 41	64
x. 12	163	vi. 1-7.	62	iv. 38	62
xii.	158	xi. 29-39	20	v. 22	63, 64
xiv. 2, 21	179	xii. 1-31	5	v. 27.	57
xv. 12, 13.	196	xii.-II. Kings iii.	3	vi. 1-7.	57, 64
xviii. 9-15	63	xii. 20.	26	vi. 23, 24.	57
xviii. 9-22	139	xii. 22-24.	20	vi. 23.	73
xxiv. 16	123	xii. 26-31	5	vi. 24-vii. 20.	73
xxvi.	163	xii. 31	6	viii. 1.	73
xxvi. 1, 9.	179	xii. 32-xiii. 32	5	viii. 1-6	57
xxviii.	163	xii. 28.	32	viii. 4, 5.	57
xxviii. 9.	179	xiii. 33, 34.	6	viii. 12.	72
xxxiii. 17	82	xiv. 1-17.	47	viii. 16-29	7
		xiv. 1-18	6	ix. 1-x. 27.	57
		xiv. 17.	35	ix. 11, 12	64
JUDGES.		xv. 1-4	10	ix. 26.	123
i. 2, 4, 8, 28.	17	xv. 17-22	27	x. 15-23.	51
v. 2, 3, 5, 7-9, 11	17	xv. 33.	35	x. 15-24.	191
xviii. 30	32	xvi. 1-4	6, 47	x. 17-28	68
xix.	90	xvi. 33, 34.	39	x. 32, 33	72
		xvii.-xix.	6	xi.-xvii.	113
		xviii.	49	xi. 1-20	113
JOSHUA.		xviii. 19, 22	62	xi. 1-xii. 21	113
vii. 24-26	123	xix. 16-21	61	xii. 4-16.	113
		xx.	6, 7, 38, 50	xii. 17, 18	113
		xx. 34.	38	xiii. 3	73
I. SAMUEL.		xx. 35-43	6, 64	xiii. 5.	74
i. 3, 9.	31	xxi.	6	xiii. 14-21	57
viii.	164	xxii.	6, 7, 49, 57, 64	xiii. 17-19.	25, 76
xi. 8	17	xxii. 1-38.	6	xiii. 20, 21.	72
xvii. 52	17	xxii. 5.	49	xiv. 1-14, 17-22	113
		xxii. 43	46	xiv. 6	123
II. SAMUEL.		**II. KINGS.**		xiv. 8-14.	58
xi. 11	17	i. 2.	15	xiv. 8-14, 19, 20, 22.	113
xii. 8.	17	i. 1-17ᵃ	6	xiv. 19.	117
xvi. 1-14.	26	i. 17ᵇ, 18.	6	xiv. 22.	123
xix. 16, 20.	26	ii.	7	xiv. 25	76, 79
xx. 1	23	ii. 3.	62	xv. 1-7, 32-38.	113
xxi.	123	ii. 5.	62	xv. 5.	113, 117
xxi. 1-22.	26	iii.	57	xv. 16	98
xxi. 2	17	iii. 1-3.	7	xv. 19.	60
xxiv. 15, 16.	150	iii. 4.	11	xv. 19, 20.	98

INDEX OF REFERENCES

	Page		Page		Page
xv. 29	101	xxv.-xxix.	142	xxviii. 7-xxix. 24	115
xv. 30	101	xxv. 1	142	xxviii. 9-13	144
xvi. 1-20	113			xxviii. 14, 15	143
xvi. 3	139	**ISAIAH.**		xxix. 4	139
xvi. 5-9	113	i.	115	xxix. 5-8	145
xvi. 7-41	58	i. 6	137	xxix. 9-14	143
xvi. 9	102	i. 7, 8	128	xxix. 15	144
xvi. 10	119	i. 10-17	139	xxx.-xxxii.	115
xvi. 10-18	113	i. 23	137	xxx. 1-4	144
xvii. 4	103	i. 29	138	xxx. 7	144
xvii. 6	106	ii. 1, 2	136	xxx. 9	143
xvii. 24	106	ii. 5-iv. 1	114	xxx. 15	143
xviii.	113	ii. 6	119, 140	xxx. 22	157
xviii. 4	138, 140, 157	ii. 8	137, 138	xxxi. 1	144
xviii. 8	141	ii. 9	137	xxxi. 3	144
xviii. 9-12	113	ii. 20	138	xxxi. 4-9	145
xviii. 10	118	iii. 2	139	xxxi. 7	157
xviii. 13	118	iii. 2, 3	137	xxxii.	154
xviii. 13-16	113	iii. 2, 3	139	xxxvi.	113, 115
xviii. 14	148	iii. 11	137	xxxvii.	113, 115
xviii. 17-xix. 37	113	iii. 12	114	xxxviii.	115
xix. 20-34	149	iii. 14, 15	137	xxxix.	115, 143
xix. 35	150	iii. 16, 17	137	xxxix. 1	118
xx. 1-6	118	v.	135		
xx. 12	118	v. 1-25	114	**JEREMIAH.**	
xx. 12-21	143	v. 22, 23	136	i. 5	175
xx. 13	141	v. 26, 30	114	i. 11-19	175
xx. 20	141	vi.	114	i. 14	176
xxi. 3, 4	161	vi. 1	129	ii.-vi.	168
xxi. 6	160	vii.-ix. 7	114	ii. 30	160
xxi. 16	160	vii. 2	128	iii. 16	203
xxi. 18, 26	125	viii. 4	132	iv. 1	176
xxi. 21	172	viii. 6	127	v. 1	176
xxii.-xxv.	167	viii. 12	132	vii.-ix.	169
xxiii.	164	viii. 16	133, 156	vii. 3-15	186
xxiii. 7	160	viii. 17, 18	133	vii. 4	186
xxiii. 9	178	viii. 19	132, 139	vii. 8	187
xxiii. 10	160	ix. 1-7	153	viii. 8, 11	187
xxiii. 11, 12	161	ix. 8-x. 4	114	x. 17-25	169
xxiii. 13	157	x. 5-xi. 9	115, 146	x. 21	185
xxiii. 29-xxiv. 1	167	xi. 1-9	154	xi. 1-8	169, 181
xxiv. 7	193	xiv. 24-27	115, 146	xi. 9-xii. 6	169
		xiv. 27	146	xi. 10	186
I. CHRONICLES.		xiv. 29	143	xi. 13	186
iii. 13	124	xiv. 29-32	115	xi. 18-23	187
		xiv. 29-31	144	xii. 7-xiii. 27	169
II. CHRONICLES.		xv.	79	xiii. 18, 19	193
xiii. 1-22	10	xvi.	79	xiv.-xx.	169
xiv.	43	xvi. 1-11	114	xvii. 2	186
xvi. 11	9	xvii. 12-14	115, 146	xvii. 5, 7	191
xvii.	43	xviii. 17-xix. 37	114	xviii. 3-12	155
xxiii.-xxxiii.	114	xix.	155	xviii. 6, 11	191
xxiv. 27	9	xix. 21-31	114	xviii. 12	191
xxv. 26	9	xx.	115	xix.	192
xxvii. 7	9	xx. 1-19	114	xx.	192
xxviii. 5-18	127	xx. 3	142	xx. 9	192
xxviii. 26	9	xxi.	114	xx. 12	192
xxxii.	147	xxii. 1-5	148	xxi. 1-10	169
xxxiii. 18	9	xxii. 1-14	115, 147	xxii. 10-12	169
xxxv. 27	9	xxii. 3	147	xxii. 13-15	185
xxxvi. 8	9	xxii. 7	147	xxii. 13-30	169
		xxii. 10	147	xxii. 15, 16	181
EZRA.		xxii. 13	148	xxii. 17	185
iv. 2, 9, 10	107	xxii. 15-25	115	xxii. 24	192
		xxviii.	115	xxii. 26	192
PROVERBS.		xxviii. 1-6	115	xxiv.	169
i.-ix.	182	xxviii. 1-13	91	xxv.	169, 188
x.-xxix.	182	xxviii. 7	143	xxv. 12	189

xxvi. 169, 187	iv. 5–9 94	v. 21–24 33
xxvi.-xxix. 169	iv. 6 90	v. 21–25 95
xxvi. 18 119	iv. 11–14 94	vi. 1–7 88
xxvi. 18, 19 157	iv. 11–15 90	vi. 4 .... 76, 88
xxvii. 195	v. 1 .... 31, 90, 100	vi. 6 88
xxvii. 16 193	v. 13 59	vi. 14 .... 91, 95
xxviii. 195	vi. 9 .... 90, 94	vii. 9 .... 68, 82
xxx.-xxxiii. 169	vii. 1 90	vii. 10–13 82
xxxi. 29, 30 203	vii. 3–7, 16 59	vii. 12, 13 .... 82, 93
xxxi. 31–34 203	vii. 5 83	vii. 14 80
xxxiv. 169, 196	vii. 5–7 90	vii. 14, 15 82
xxxv. 51, 169	vii. 8 59	vii. 15 80
xxxvi. 190	vii. 8–16 100	viii. 1–3 86
xxxvi. 1–8 169	vii. 11 .... 59, 99, 100	viii. 4 88
xxxvi. 32 170	viii. 2 93	viii 5 90
xxxvi. 168, 190	viii. 5 96	ix. 7 95
xxxvi. 9–32 169	viii. 9 59	ix. 8–15 90
xxxvii. 169, 197	viii. 14 83	ix. 9, 10 157
xxxvii. 5 196	ix. 1–5 94	
xxxviii. 169	ix. 7 85	**Micah.**
xxxiv.-xliv. 170	ix. 8 85	i.-iii. 116
xl. 1 .... 199, 200	ix. 9 90	i. 1 7 116
xlv. 1–xlix. 33 169	x. 4 90	i. 1, 14 126
xlvi. 188	x. 5 96	i. 2–7 91
xlvi. 188	x. 6, 9, 10 83	i. 10–16 123
xlix. 34–39 169	x. 9 90	i. 13. 140
l. 169	x. 15 59	ii. 12, 13 116
li. 169	xi. 1 83	iii. 5 .... 82, 139
li. 59 169	xi. 1–4 97	iii. 7 139
lii. 170	xi. 8, 9 97	iii. 11 139
lii. 30 201	xi. 9 152	iii. 12 .... 156, 187
lii. 31–34 193	xi. 12 90	iv. 116
	xii. 1 100	v. 116, 159
Lamentations.	xii. 11 59	v. 3–6 154
ii. 19–22 198	xii. 12 83	vi. 1–vii. 6 116
iv. 10 198	xiii. 2, 3 96	vi. 6, 7 160
iv. 20 193	xiii. 4 83	vi. 6–8 139
	xiii. 16 91	vi. 8 161
Ezekiel.	xiv. 3, 4 96	vii. 116
i. 2 193		
i. 3 193	**Amos.**	**Habakkuk.**
i.-vii. 170	i. 79, 94	ii. 4 189
viii. 194	i.-iii. 88	ii. 8 189
viii.-xix. 170	i. 1 79	
viii. 12 194	i. 3, 4 72	**Zephaniah.**
ix. 9 194	i. 6–15 72	i. 4–6 174
xvii. 15 196	i. 12 123	i. 12 174
xx.-xxiii. 170	ii. 80, 94	ii. 174
xxiv. 170	ii. 6, 7 88	ii. 3 174
xxiv. 21 193	ii. 7 90	iii. 3, 4 174
xxv.-xxxii. 170	ii. 8 33	iii. 13, 20 175
	iii. 2 95	
Daniel.	iii. 3–8 81	**Zechariah.**
i. 2 193	iii. 9 90	xiv. 5 13
v. 2 193	iii. 9, 10 80	
	iii. 10 89	**Moabite Stone.**
Hosea.	iii. 11, 12 88	4–6. 38
i.-iii. 58	iv. 2 152	
i. 4 .... 68, 83	iv. 4 31	**Sargon Cylinder Inscription.**
i. 4–9 132	iv. 4, 5 .... 33, 95	
ii. 9–23 90	iv. 6–11 .... 72, 92	29 143
ii. 10–23 97	iv. 12 91	
iii. 3, 4 91	v. 2 90	**Taylor Prism Inscription.**
iii. 4, 5 97	v. 11 88	ii. 44–57 145
iv.-xiv. 58	v. 12 89	iii. 32 147
iv. 1, 2 89	v. 18 93	

For Product Safety Concerns and Information please contact our EU representative GPSR@taylorandfrancis.com
Taylor & Francis Verlag GmbH, Kaufingerstraße 24, 80331 München, Germany